Devotional Rhyme

Volume II

POEMS OF HOPE, LOVE, AND INSPIRATION
STRAIGHT F...

J. Luke McClellan

TRILOGY CHRISTIAN PUBLISHERS
Tustin, CA

Trilogy Christian Publishers
A Wholly Owned Subsidiary of Trinity Broadcasting Network
2442 Michelle Drive
Tustin, CA 92780

Devotional Rhyme, Volume II: Poems of Hope, Love and Inspiration, Straight from a God-Filled Heart

Copyright © 2024 by J. Luke McClellan

Scripture quotations marked (NIV) are taken from THE HOLY BIBLE, NEW INTERNATIONAL VERSION®, NIV® Copyright © 1973, 1978, 1984, 2011 by Biblica, Inc.® Used by permission. All rights reserved worldwide.

All rights reserved, including the right to reproduce this book or portions thereof in any form whatsoever.

For information, address Trilogy Christian Publishing

Rights Department, 2442 Michelle Drive, Tustin, Ca 92780.

Trilogy Christian Publishing/TBN and colophon are trademarks of Trinity Broadcasting Network.

For information about special discounts for bulk purchases, please contact Trilogy Christian Publishing.

Trilogy Disclaimer: The views and content expressed in this book are those of the author and may not necessarily reflect the views and doctrine of Trilogy Christian Publishing or the Trinity Broadcasting Network.

10 9 8 7 6 5 4 3 2 1

Library of Congress Cataloging-in-Publication Data is available.

ISBN 979-8-89333-281-0

ISBN 979-8-89333-282-7 (ebook)

Introduction

Picking up where "Volume I" left off, "Devotional Rhyme, Volume II" is an ambitious foray into the realms of darkness often experienced, but rarely discussed by most individuals.

It unabashedly proclaims that all unwanted thoughts, feelings and experiences are placed, set forth and facilitated by none other than evil, for which is destroyed by none other than the purveyor of all good—God.

So, with that idea in mind, behold the inner-workings of a brain that has suffered much. Yet, despite that suffering, has made it to the other side, but only due to God's help, as this book details that very spoken-of journey. You are not alone.

J. Luke McClellan

January First

The cycles of anxiety, continue to write me
Back into my evil book of traps
In fact I recoil, at the blood in me that boils
As I'm mad at myself for just that
Wishing to escape, the pain in this place
What strategy can I possible apply?
My tactics have failed, as all that prevails
Is serving God to fulfill me in this life

Devotional Rhyme

January Second

The thunder that cracks, as I traverse on this road
The lightening is blindingly bright
My life is a confusing clash, as I try to get back home
I've been gone far too long to recognize
So how can my eyes, readjust to a life
Serving God as the only thought on my mind
The truth is He's called me, to absolve me from the chains
That have constrained me in the name of Jesus Christ

J. Luke McClellan

January Third

The dreams of us as warriors
Are the dreams up in the stars
The beings that were here before us
Are what set us all apart
For they sacrificed more for us
Than we could ever do as we are
But the divinity within we
Echoes peace, in Christ, in heart

January Fourth

I set the tone when I'm perplexed alone
I feel my solitude cave in
My isolation is a nice vacation
From the ways in which I've sinned
But the truth I used to think and use
Are the views of women and men
Common folk, are robbin' hope
Only Christ can save us, my friends

J. Luke McClellan

January Fifth

I see the writing in plain English
It's such a beautiful pathway to learn
But the language is demeaning itself
As the words that are used only hurt
We talk about our lives as we write
Expert scribes, only lies, unsure
But if we can seek He without all the falsity
We exemplify peaceful times that will be heard

January Sixth

Frozen like a moment in time I can't escape
What is this dread that I indulge?
Maybe I should take a second to relate
To the fact that my thoughts are escaping me; divulged
As my mind is like a ticking time bomb's fate
This simply isn't leaving me replete; full
My pieces are shattered, my life's a disaster
But with God this crisis is annulled

J. Luke McClellan

January Seventh

The buildings around me
Are disintegrating like burnt paper to ash
What is this experience as my horror show?
I know that these things
Aren't ever going to last
But the truth is God is what is shown
When the obstructions and distractions
And calluses of life
Are removed and guess who is still there
God the Father
And Jesus the Christ
Being the constants that always have cared

Devotional Rhyme

January Eighth

These thoughts are deeply swallowed
As my mind becomes hollow
Never again will I love
But if I still look to tomorrow
I'll be given a new hope so
I can confide in all that He does

J. Luke McClellan

January Ninth

I know the end
Is just the beginning
Look to the sky for clarity
Feeling the seeping
My evil thoughts leaving
As I once could barely see
But now I feel God
And Christ too entering
As my mind's alive in He
This is my time
To embrace the divine
This is God, Jesus and me

January Tenth

I am empowered
By the love in God's touch
I can feel His caress on my cheek
And know that with each hour
That passes by with such
Haste, anxiety and speed
Time is just a concept
That is foreign to God
A premise only understood by He
But with faith unperplexed
I know just what to expect
I'm absolved; that is all; I'm complete

J. Luke McClellan

January Eleventh

A sudden rush has overtaken me
I'm alone, isolated, incomplete
The void that fills my heart is empty
A paradox but introspection I seek
So what is it I need to fill me up
To fulfill the warmth I long to give
The depth of my soul is more than enough
With God, I've my purpose to live

Devotional Rhyme

January Twelfth

May these times find us at peace with what is
A heart can be troubled and break
But if deciding to take a new way to live
In Christ, your heart's healed, from the ache

January Thirteenth

The snow covers the wounds in the flesh
The body is dormant, stiff, cold
The mind is fatigued from the truth confessed
The heart feels what the brain already knows
As the ice forms frost on the lip, covering tongue
It speaks no more; it is still
May your thoughts glorify Christ as the one
Whose miracles each moment are revealed

January Fourteenth

The ocean waves have washed upon the shore
A dying heart that is forever lost
May the sun rays create a new folklore
The truth that was missed in thought
So a new horizon is evident and present
As the sand becomes salt of the sea
And when I stand up to face the change in my essence
I hear the Word of God speak to me

J. Luke McClellan

January Fifteenth

A shift in tone has become my home
Change is always present here
I never know when someone will go
And leave me to die, it's become clear
That the heart of society, has shifted, decayed
Morality is a thing of the past
But I own this, I'm equipped, I know my ways
With God, my humanity can last

January Sixteenth

These markings on my skin signify renewal
As my plans fade away into dusk
My fate seems to be stopping what I came here to do
Now, I create, a new must
And that idea so it seems is relinquishing
I didn't think would be possible, but guess what
God is my inspiration for this life at stake
And the only one that I trust

J. Luke McClellan

January Seventeenth

I have mastered nothing
As I realize something
My faith is all that matters now
For God is the one being
The constant everything
That I need to find my way out

Devotional Rhyme

January Eighteenth

Shower me with all your love, Lord
For I am weak and in peril
And I'm unworthy to be with thee, Lord
I surrender to the wisdom you herald
And I find that my time isn't worthy of life
If it doesn't involve you by my side
So please accept my offering, bringing you lost souls
thought to be
Forgotten, but not in this time

January Nineteenth

I'm seeing a new darkness in myself
This world has beaten me down
Feeling impoverished and stripped of my wealth
I unjustly am wearing a shameful crown
As the people here used to make me think
That I was somebody original to them
But they turned their backs, proving I'm not unique
Yet, to God and Christ, I am

Devotional Rhyme

January Twentieth

When the time comes for me to face my fate
The one in my life I create
I know I'll concede the truth that you read
In Jesus the Christ, I am saved

January Twenty-First

I see that the pain that's in me is me
Nothing else deeper than that
And if I think that I need to be free
I look again back at my trap
There's nothing to escape as the peace in this life
Is within me to find as I need
The calling of Christ, together we try
And achieve all I couldn't achieve

Devotional Rhyme

January Twenty-Second

My thoughts are so daunting as I lift up my head
Wishing I could make them go away
But the truth of the matter isn't fixed, it is said
In Christ I can be healed of my pain
So why, oh why, do I need to be denied
When it's clear that my malaise is in vein
Not so fast, as I get back on track
At peace, in God, I'm okay

January Twenty-Third

I realize some of the things in my past
Were reflections of self-loathing projected
I couldn't process, compute or do the math
That my life had been subjected
To deception, evil, bitterness and hate
All dwellings of the devil, as expected
The prince of darkness thriving on pain
But overcome, in Christ, I'm protected

Devotional Rhyme

January Twenty-Fourth

Descending upon ending this life as an envy
There's nothing more unfulfilling than that
I'm ready to be steady with my heavy heart aplenty
With God's warmth and love, I am back

J. Luke McClellan

January Twenty-Fifth

Such a sweet serenity
A scene that was divinely arranged
God has designed a life for our lives
And provided what's needed, the same

January Twenty-Sixth

Don't overthink the wonders of He
As God is the grand-architect of wisdom
He knows all, controls all and shows all His peace
Never changes, with each moment by Him, given

J. Luke McClellan

January Twenty-Seventh

Painting a blue, hue or two
Or three, could be green or pink
Yellow stripes, not quite subdued
Then again, maybe, what you think?
I don't think, I just breathe, on knees
Pressing my hands, follow me
The blessings of Christ as He provides
My prayers are both heard and received

January Twenty-Eighth

I believe in something so magnificent
There's a lift in my step when I walk
It has nothing to do with my actions spent
Living in a world of thought
God is what's present in my life as it's
The reason that I love to talk
Bringing my people to their knees under steeples
I know why by God I was brought

J. Luke McClellan

January Twenty-Ninth

A demonic presence
Can be felt here at home
Like the beat of this world, dark, in pain
But with God, it's evident
You will never be alone
With Him you are free from the shame

January Thirtieth

I seek to be at peace with me
There is no ease achieved
I think I need to reach for me
But leave the "me"; agreed
I know all right, begins with Christ
God is indeed, the Divine
The name so great, I thank each night
Jesus Christ, I rhyme

J. Luke McClellan

January Thirty-First

Despite the pain
Inside of my brain
I find my peace within God
I hope and I pray
Letting go of the day
Christ is my staff and rod

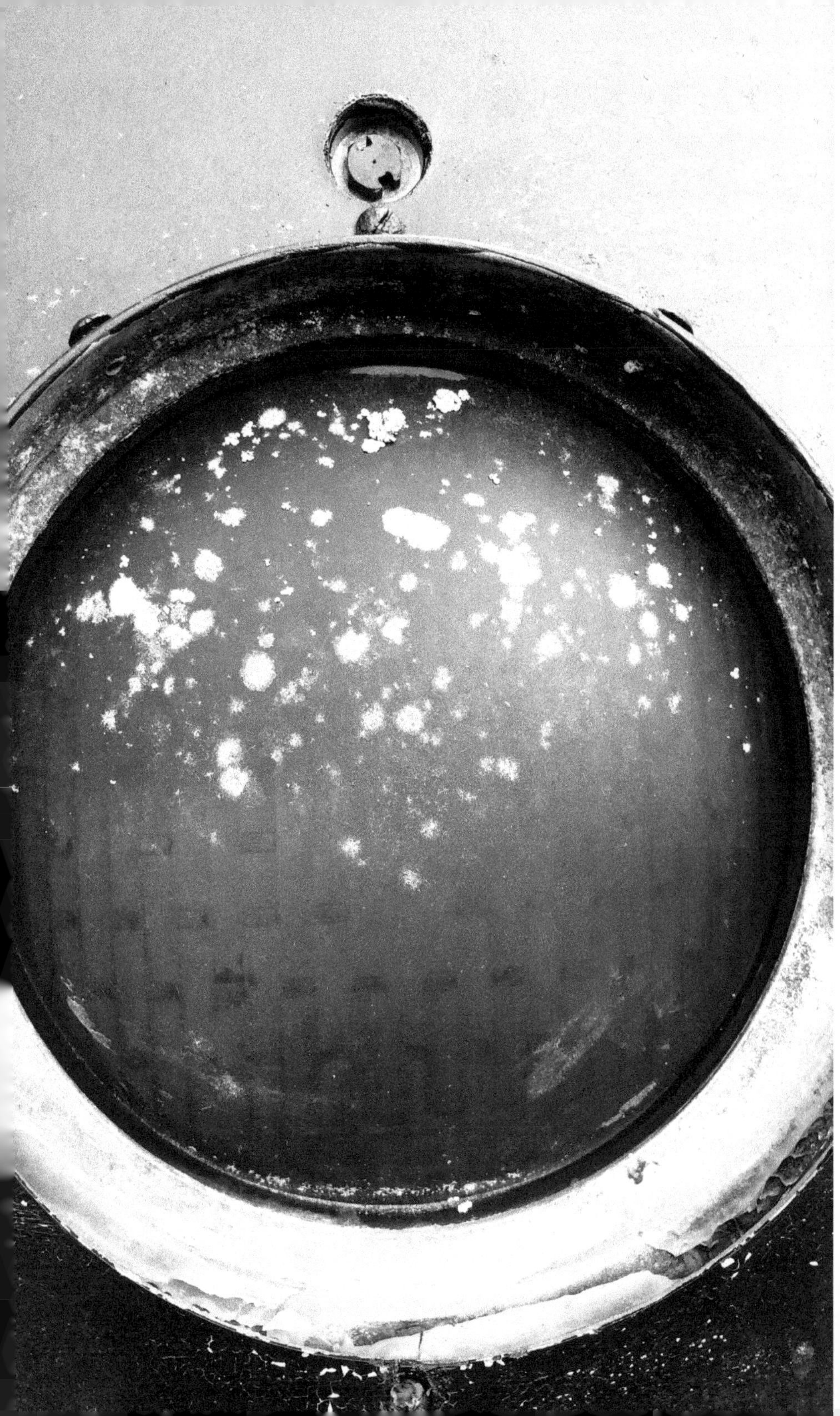

J. Luke McClellan

February First

Quiet whispers haunt me
Coming to me, they descend
When I'm with myself, honestly
I feel as though I cannot depend
On the light of this world provided at night
There is no truth to this end
The wisdom I seek is embedded in me
A life with God's light shall begin

February Second

The business of the day
Is shrouded in gray
I know my soul screams for relief
But when I look God's way
I discover through my pain
In Christ, I can find my peace

February Third

Never again, will I say I'm a friend
When I know good and well what that means
It's a commitment I'm pretending that I'm vested in
But the truth is I'm too much about me
No wonder I'm so empty, as my tank is on E
I can no longer struggle to bare
The torment of this world, rooted so deeply
But God has always been there

February Fourth

∽

I roam empty streets
With the flashing of lights
Bright and yet so dim
Lacking capacity
When in actuality
Christ is the lane we should ride in

∽

J. Luke McClellan

February Fifth

These chains that whip me
Confine my state
Making me disappear
I wish to be the epitome
Of a man who has changed
But I'm without a mind that's clear
And here I sit and rest
Idle to become stale
Yet suddenly remember the truth
That God still expects
Me to lift up; prevail
I know in Him, this, I can do

February Sixth

Such a rush to get
When living without sin
But my fallacy is myself each day
I understand that I live
In a painful den
When I forget all Jesus Christ's ways
So I abandon the idea
Of being of this life
And learning to be at peace with love
Jesus heals my lies
And sets my tone right
Changing the ways which I conduct

J. Luke McClellan

February Seventh

I see the truth
God is my way
Jesus has healed my errors
I used to be used
By these people each day
But with God and Christ, I am better

February Eighth

Does it make a difference
When each day is the same?
What's the point in continuing on?
I see my appearance
As being a man who's changed
But I know what I know and when wrong
So who can be my witness?
As I want to correct my mistakes
I fear that all hope is gone
Jesus believes I can live this
The way of His ways
So I feel His strength make me strong

J. Luke McClellan

February Ninth

I see the difference in me
I don't need this place
These people aren't the ones for my life
Jesus Christ believes
That I can be a man of change
So I seek out His ways and live right

February Tenth

When the change we seek
Is placed at our feet
We fail to understand God's ways
But the kindness we believe
That exists as anomalies
In Christ, it becomes how we change

February Eleventh

I'm hearing a new tone that mellows my cerebrum
I've decided this is where I should stay
I would never go question God's Divine reason
I accept; I am still; I remain

February Twelfth

The terror inside my mind is a thousand times worse
Than any reality for which I could live
This pain is diseased which resides inside me
As I want to take back what I did
And I know that I think, I obsess and lose sleep
But believe that I've so much to give
As the peace that's inside me, is brought out abundantly
Christ was, will be and is

J. Luke McClellan

February Thirteenth

I make mistakes daily
I live in sin
I'm a travesty to the image I see
But with God, I'm not failing
And instead I can win
As Christ had intended for me

February Fourteenth

May you find your way
When you're lost in the woods
As God's light will always be bright
He understands your pain
And all of your "shoulds"
But with Him, you can set moments right

February Fifteenth

May the days of rain pour down with hope
May the pain that behaves in a way which provokes
While evening is clear and the days here unknown
God is the light, that is bright, which you chose

February Sixteenth

Decisions are visions met with uncertainty
But finally find their way out
God is the essence of benevolence and mercy
By which His Grace you are allowed

February Seventeenth

Talking to myself I believe I need help
Where is God to give me a reprieve?
I need some relief from the being of me
And I pray as I think I'm diseased
But endeavor to treasure discovering peace
Wishing for me that I'm free
Look at what's happened, I react to the actions
That God has set before me

February Eighteenth

I realize that the time in our lives
Is spent to get somewhere else
We all wish that we could just buy
That thing that gleams on the shelf
Or maybe it's affection that we think is the blessing
That we need to be with ourselves
But the truth is, I tell you, God is who helps you
He is the fulfillment that dwells

J. Luke McClellan

February Nineteenth

I don't know
What the future holds
But I do know with God, it is good
He'll always show
The truth to behold
He is the essence of "could"

February Twentieth

My faith on this day
Has made me well
My mistakes I forsake
And refuse to dwell
My heartbeat is hardly
A mistake; excels
I will take God's ways
As a sign of His help

J. Luke McClellan

February Twenty-First

My health is well
When I live in God
But I felt life was hell
Trapped in my thoughts
And I escaped my cell
When I said they could rot
And went back to dwell
In a life full of God

February Twenty-Second

Life's mysteries continue to leave me
Suspecting what I never dreamed
I feel as though God's angel was sent to me
To help me overcome thoughts I think
And I know that I can and will be
At peace in God at ease
This is quite frankly all I'll ever need
In He and Christ I'm complete

J. Luke McClellan

February Twenty-Third

My malaise has taken days
Even weeks for me to find peace
It seems to be a chronic thing
For my pain to be felt when I speak
But I know the truth in ways
For me to be at ease
God and Christ the Duo of Divine
My life, my all, I'll be

February Twenty-Fourth

Maybe I should savor the moments I know
Are my best and cherish what they are
I'm confident though, my truth will be known
When I accept God and Christ for who they are

J. Luke McClellan

February Twenty-Fifth

The blessings by which I've decided are gifts
Directly from God up above
I seek Him to live; the purest to exist
Jesus, you are who I love

February Twenty-Sixth

⁂

When the pain becomes the bane of your existence
Remember this: God is your help
No shame no blame just purely acceptance
That Christ went through more than you've felt
And I know that you want something more than you have
Believe me, we all feel this too
But God gives us strength, in adversity's way
With Christ, there's no stopping the truth

⁂

February Twenty-Seventh

No computers here; just a simple mind relaxed
No technology to fear; at peace, at ease with that
God is all who steers; nothing complicated; fact
Jesus Christ is here; saved; no going back

February Twenty-Eighth

Simple equations are making my head spin
Why does life seem so hard?
I find the relation between peace and salvation
One in the same in God's heart

February Twenty-Ninth

May the continuation of time
Find you in divine
Leading a life committed to Christ
And discover all your woes
For which we all know
Can be absolved with He in our lives

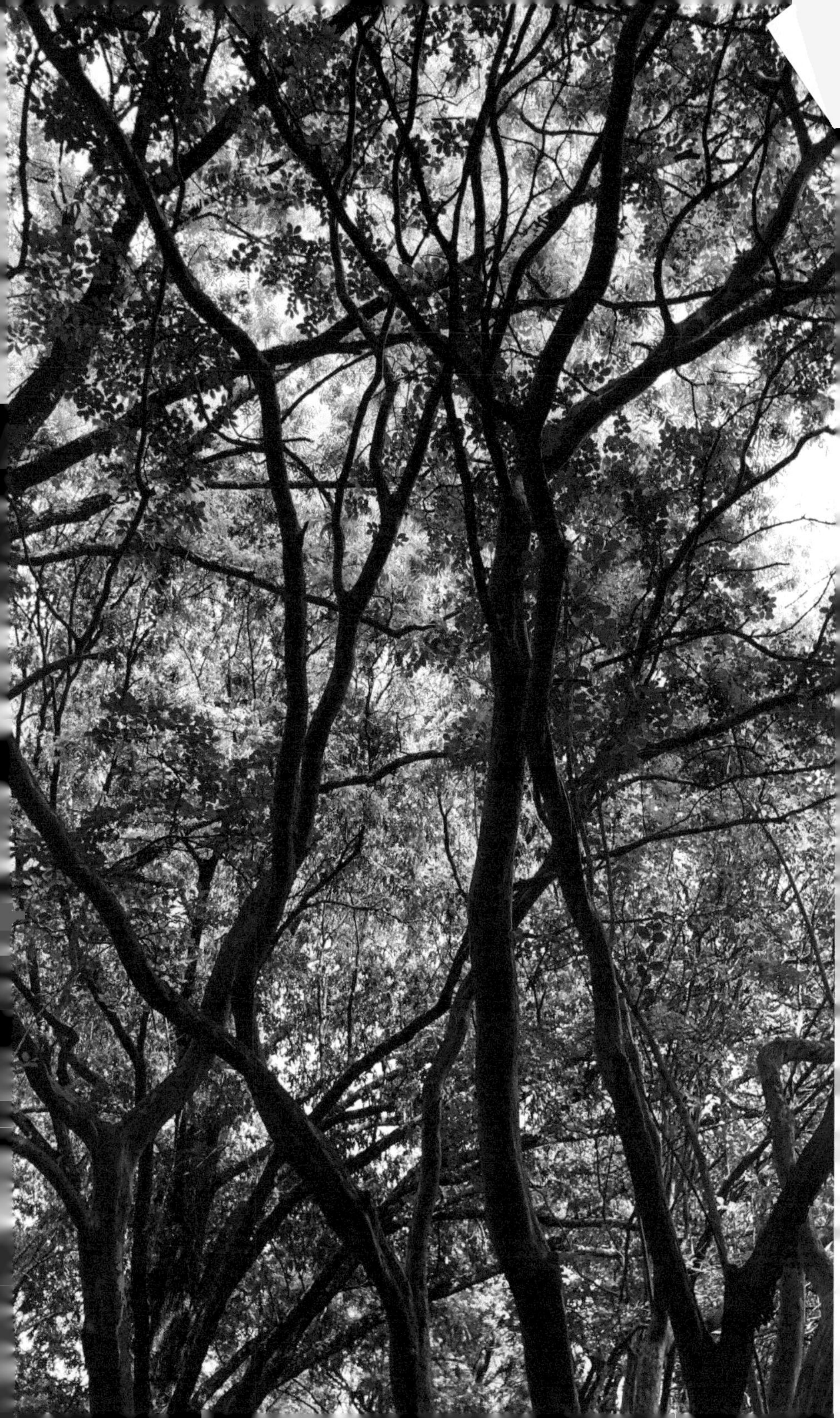

J. Luke McClellan

March First

The wind blows all directions
But clearly there's one
That guides us back to God's light
His name equates to salvation
And He's already come
He is called Jesus the Christ

March Second

Accepting that the control is out of my hands
Is the best thing for my life I can do
The peace that I seek is inside; I can
But only with God this I choose

March Third

The chatter of birds is after my heart
The way that they're heard, is quite frankly art
The benevolence of God is the essence of who we are
And through He, we can be at peace, when life's hard

March Fourth

The quiet is quite divine when it's inter-
twined with rhymes of God
And I find my lines of time define, my best
reflective thoughts
Forever to better the weather that severs the
never we said that we got
Jesus Christ, He healed my strife, He is the
one I sought

March Fifth

My confession is I'm addicted to Jesus
I never for a second thought I would speak this
Many years ago, my life was in pieces
But now I seek Him; for He is my thesis
Amen.

March Sixth

It depends on the day
For the light of God's rays
To impact how I react to my pain
I look to Him first
As I'm renewed in Christ's birth
And will never again see my life as the same

J. Luke McClellan

March Seventh

I know that the silence we have
Is a way to speak when we're mad
Maybe we can set our differences aside
Let's look to God's glory
And tell all our story
That in God, we made peace, leaving resentment behind

March Eighth

My motto is to bottle all my emotion
Without thought, so
I'll leave all the pain I have behind
If only it were that simple
But when thanking the Lord for His literal
Blessings He's bestowed; all is fine

J. Luke McClellan

March Ninth

The gift of gab is a rift; a jab
I get that you're sad when you're behind
But don't let the gloom, overtake you
In God and Christ, peace, you can find

March Tenth

The electronics in my mind have become part of my life
In fact they've overtaken how I live
But if I forget the pretense and go back to another time
Peace in God can be, what is

J. Luke McClellan

March Eleventh

My headache has dissipated as has the pain in my side
I know what's created this fix
Making my prayers up to God to be heard, never to deny
As He mercifully resolves my conflict

March Twelfth

The perils of life
Conflict my mind
Where shall I go when I fail?
When I herald divine,
It makes sense in time
God is my strength that prevails

J. Luke McClellan

March Thirteenth

I seek to find a peace in me
But I return adrift, bereft and departed
But when in Christ I confide my needs
His hand heals all the injuries, I started

March Fourteenth

My eyes feel heavy; tired; asleep
Yet I'm walking in pace with this day
I wish I could arrive, with alertness to think
And with God, is achieved, when I pray

J. Luke McClellan

March Fifteenth

Our time in this life is limited by design
As God wanted for us, a finite pulse-line
But the pulls to Divine, never dull to the mind
As God and Christ will always provide

March Sixteenth

Temptations aren't always apparent
In the guise of humankind
But this is the devil's lecherous hint
To convince with the very hope it
Makes us all forget in mind
That we were put here by God's omnipotence
So how do we prevent all this
Such sinful, falling events
From occurring as we are working each day
Dismiss living in satan's sin
And get our minds back to Him
"Him" being Christ our God, the one who saves

J. Luke McClellan

March Seventeenth

May the calm in your mind
Pronounce itself loud
May you hear the whisper of God in heart
May you find peace in time
With Him calling you now
Christ is the root of renewed starts

March Eighteenth

Calm can be found in the wind that blows
Thoughts can stir about creating a hold
Gripping you tight, but it's best to let go
Know that in Christ your life can be whole

March Nineteenth

Think of peace and peace you shall have
But what equates to peace in this life?
Jesus, so believe it that He is the max
You can feel when you're alive

March Twentieth

I think the hollow holes in my heart
Represent the void I desire to fill
I wish I knew more of what's caused me to depart
From the center of God as my will
And I know that I'll go and foolishly hold
The things I think this life can bring
There's isn't a peace in reality it's just He
Jesus Christ as Salvation's King

March Twenty-First

Which path shall put me back
On track to get relaxed
I think it's the Prince of Peace
His name is Christ
And please believe He's my
Everything and all that I need

March Twenty-Second

I find myself buried in a landfill of waste
Wishing I could escape this pit
The debris that's in me is my own fate
As I've chosen my way; written it
But I sense a change, inside my brain
A stirring is creating the right fit
Unquestionably cemented, I know I'm forgiven
In Christ, I bow down and submit

J. Luke McClellan

March Twenty-Third

Jesus has chosen me
To travel on the road to be
Meeting His love, making it mine
And I know I will go to be
The one who grows in He
Sharing this love with all whom I find

March Twenty-Fourth

I have discovered
That my place in this life
Is making space for the grace of Christ
And all my mistakes
Have no way to lie
As in Him I'm given new life

J. Luke McClellan

March Twenty-Fifth

With all that I do
I find that the blues
Inevitably creep in to overtake
In time He will prove
That all I need to use
Is accepting Jesus as the way

March Twenty-Sixth

I look to the stars
Call up to God
And ask for healing of this pain
I know He's not far
He knows I am lost
And in Him I am healed without shame

J. Luke McClellan

March Twenty-Seventh

The merit of my actions
Is actually in fashion
My math is accurate in this
The fact when I happen
To give God my passion
All pain in my life, then vanishes

March Twenty-Eighth

I find this pain
To be indescribably mundane
It's insane these thoughts from my brain
But with the help of Christ
I can overcome all life's strife
And place my faith in His name

J. Luke McClellan

March Twenty-Ninth

The homeopathic remedies
Are simply the pathway to God
He built them to complete our journey
The accessibility that we seek
Is indeed provided by He
And there's no other road to deter me

March Thirtieth

I trust in God
With all my thoughts
He reminds me to be at ease
I know He's my rock
As I develop new plots
And seek to complete my time; free

J. Luke McClellan

March Thirty-First

I'm troubled in my mind
There's a war being waged
I wish to have talks of peace
But when I get right
With God as my way
I find that the battle has ceased

J. Luke McClellan

April First

The fear of my pain has a burdening grip
The shallow depths of the darkness can overshadow
and eclipse
All of my walks, travels, galore
But my home is with God and nothing more

April Second

These tenuous times
Imbue a divine
Intervention we feel isn't fair
But the truth of the rhyme
Is this isn't our minds
It's God's decision to direct just where

April Third

The sparkle in your eye
Indicates you're alive
Welcome to this existence by God
Embrace the warmth of divine
As you're living this life
May Christ consume your every thought

April Fourth

The difficulties I face
Make me isolate my pain
And wish for something new
I wish to replace
The times I'd forsake
And abandon the mansion of truth
But I know that God still loves me
Even though I am ugly
In the way that I disguise my views
So I will uncover all of me
To discover I utterly
Only wish to, by God, be used

April Fifth

I suddenly feel redemption
As how I want to be mentioned
In the words that Christ speaks of me
I know Jesus believes in me
So I should too of He
And seek to be filled up with His peace

April Sixth

The swamps and marsh
Stomp out my heart
As I think I am complete in society
But they don't know they are
Dumbfounded and apart
As the pain they explain is anxiety
So look up to Him
For forgiveness of sin
By "Him" I mean Jesus Christ, my Lord
No fear to offend
As you offer the same to them
Speak the truth, as God always wants more

J. Luke McClellan

April Seventh

It seems logical to think
That this is it, complete
The end is a blackness of infinity
But how could this be
When the planets all need
A force that is of course called "gravity"
As only a divine being
Could create such fine things
In fact, it's more than me, you or any
Of us can comprehend
As only God understands
So accept this as fact; reality

April Eighth

Seek to speak the things you need
Follow the road to God
Think and ink the peace; believe
I know what I know, it's a lot
Never allow the fowl of the crowd
To diminish your belief in Christ
Silence, not violence is exactly just how
Follow Him; He is what's right

J. Luke McClellan

April Ninth

My destiny awaits
As I contemplate my faith
My ways are the ways of a sinner
And at last when I pray
He hears and explains
In Him, I'm forgiven and much bigger
Than I ever thought to be
As deep inside of me
Was a trigger of emotion to explode
But not anymore; peace
Has now become part of things
I seek as I stay on His road

April Tenth

God's plan
Is His way of making sure I stay focused on Him
God's plan
Is the name I take for granted but am forgiven
God's plan
Is the break I get when I'm sick of dealing with bad intentions
God's plan
Is the plan I need to achieve the peace I used to fail to mention

J. Luke McClellan

April Eleventh

The blessings are rolling, extolling my faith
God is so good; He's my life
I write and I pray, I decided the same
Christ is the way to get by

April Twelfth

This pain is so deep that I'm cut from tip to hilt
The blade has been lodged in for some time
I'm finding that I'm writhing, for this, I wasn't built
But the truth in Christ, is mine

April Thirteenth

~

Setting aside, for the time my mind
I find that I'm at peace when in God
Thinking and eating, simply just being
Christ is my life in my thoughts

~

April Fourteenth

The art form of self-discipline
Is a hard door to open
Maybe I should get back to kicking in
The ones shut that are closed when
The ways I live this life, are simply built in
The pain I say isn't a known friend
But truth be told, it's all I know
Until I confide my life in Him

April Fifteenth

The way that I pray I find I'm in Christ
The essence of peace within
My mind can sometimes divide up my time
But the truth I seek is in Him
So why do I derail myself and need help
When I simply, unequivocally am forgiven
My love and received grace are enough to replace
The pain that I claim as my end

April Sixteenth

This poetry exists in His presence
God sees to it you know your worth
Never forget, a child, you're of His
Forever remember these words

J. Luke McClellan

April Seventeenth

The shadows of trees
And wandering of beings
Illuminated by the moon's light
Allowing to see
Thousands of things
That only God could have created tonight

April Eighteenth

Your perspective has shifted as your life has rearranged
Don't drift too far from the dream
God to you has given, as you've always prayed
So much more to come than you think

J. Luke McClellan

April Nineteenth

The columns have fallen
The earth has cracked
And your foundation is nothing but rubble
But when you go call Him
Careful not to get sidetracked
As He sees you through all these troubles

April Twentieth

Where on earth
Is my respite that's deserved
I'm entitled to greatness I can't speak
My mindset is time to get
What I haven't yet earned
I know exactly what is owed to me
But then an unsettling
Feeling of discomfort
Washes over head-top to feet
Now I know
That God is control
And I'm too scared to any other way think

J. Luke McClellan

April Twenty-First

∽

The pulsating of my heartbeat
Has been taking my breath away artfully
I already know what this means
God, my friends has got to be
The thought in me as I honestly
Am accomplishing each one of my dreams

∽

April Twenty-Second

Where are my spring-time leaves in bloom?
Nowhere to be found in the dead of winter
Where can I go when I feel I've lost truth?
Nowhere as defeat of the fallen live here
And so to me it seems that I'm doomed
Perhaps I should end this as I enter
The darkness alone as no one here knows
Me, "accept" God; remembered

April Twenty-Third

This fever has become the heat that I can't withstand
So why do I continue to be
My apprehensions and ascensions of my self-worth are built in "can"
As I continue to focus on "me"
No, don't, you will not offer help
This time is mine to be free
But the truth I don't hear is the thoughts that I've feared
There's more to this life than just what I see
And now I can allow the moments of doubt
To exist only as mentions of possibility
God is as concrete as the wall that befalls my speech
So it is, as it was, we are in need
Let's listen to Him speaking
As His silence is beyond any of these things that we seek
Yes, God is the definition of perfection in liberty
He is our identity from our minds to our heartbeat

April Twenty-Fourth

I feel the depth of the crowds
When I'm perplexed; feeling fowl
So why am I not allowed to express
This pain I can't explain
It's unrelated to my ways
It's something much deeper than I guessed
So yes I can overcome, if I limit it to one
Thing at a time, I'll be fine
The expectations are greater than
Anything in my comprehension
As I can only achieve salvation in Christ

J. Luke McClellan

April Twenty-Fifth

I keep pressing forward only to find I revert back
To the ways that I parlayed life here before
With nothing left to gamble; no more change to bet
I'm out and have become sunk in this pit of self-remorse
So where from here to turn as my esteem has been burned
I think I could go there once more
But that is not truth as God has come to
My rescue when He knocks at my mind's door

April Twenty-Sixth

The skin is deep but the flesh can burn
I wither away in the cold
My heart double beats, my thoughts are concerned
But I know in this life I will grow old
Tired and weary, slipping away
Is there anyone left to console?
Infinity is within me when I seek He aplenty
I am saved, in Christ, as foretold

J. Luke McClellan

April Twenty-Seventh

A spring of desire is my greatest hope
I perpetuate what feels good tonight
Inevitably it will end in disaster I know
But I have to partake to get by
So why oh why does addiction's tight rope
Strangulate my efforts to try
To escape this wasteland of hate and the damned
Only God can heal this sick life

April Twenty-Eighth

I feel a force of nature take hold
What is this magnetic pull to God
Why am I drawn; sucked in so
As my life isn't going how I thought
But maybe I should consider the signs apparent
Heed the warning and yield
Absorb the message that evidently is affecting
How I live my life; He's revealed

J. Luke McClellan

April Twenty-Ninth

The children we love are God's blessings from above
He wants us to care for them all
He loves and cherishes our time with them
But He also redirects us to call
On Him when we sin and live to pretend
Never again to evolve
God is our focus; He is our hope with
Decisions we make; never fall

April Thirtieth

Earth is our playground to hurt and stay around
The choices we make are bold
Every breath we take, and step we make
We change the impact; so behold
Consider the life of Christ before He died
It's evident He self-sacrificed by Divine
God is our Healer; making us feel near home
And for that, we peacefully confide

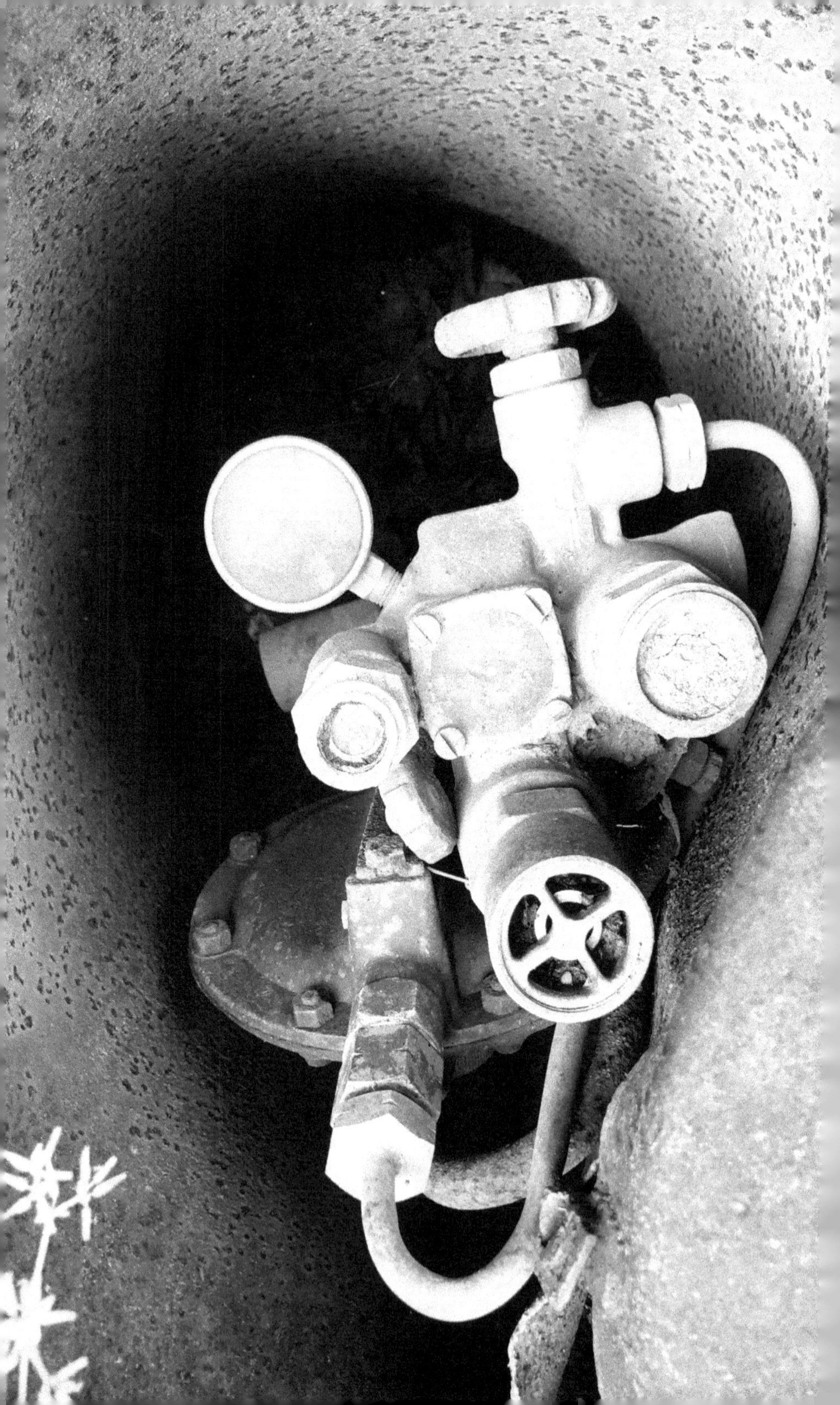

May First

I am getting impatient with the way time goes
I'm lost in wishing things were different
I need to practice being actively on hold
Accepting what comes as it is and isn't
I know that this life can be exceptionally complex
But nothing I try seems to take mold
Except my faith for which God does say:
"Go; seek; and bring all to me that you know."

May Second

The emotions can overtake and make your
thoughts ruminate
Convey in a way you're ashamed
But the day is still young and you too can join; come
Along God's path to pray

May Third

Such a deep meaning when you think you've stopped thinking
But the truth is strictly one thought at a time
No more words demeaning, offending, repeating
God is in you; peace; Divine

J. Luke McClellan

May Fourth

My maker is God
And Savior is Christ
These two are the two that fulfill
My ways away are lost
My actions can divide
But with truth; in Them; I am real

May Fifth

Heaven can seem distant
But I haven't been there yet
Maybe I should wait to be greeted by Him
Yet, I am wishing to get this
But can't as my behavior is set
Not true, but I'm who will or won't be let in
And I know my ways can change
My heart's deep-red; opaque
As I can be free from the disease of my sin
My thoughts are now at ease
Arguably or impossibly
But in God and Christ; life begins

J. Luke McClellan

May Sixth

Today I've been touched
By the power of death
A force of strength imposing weakness
And I sense my run
Of feeling energy left
Is a feeling that's fleeting; I'm defeated
Tears spill out like torn flesh's blood
Of the love I formerly exuded
With the heart's pounding of each beat that was needed
But as God's tender, benevolent, loving warmth was
Felt from the heart of my inner-most depths
He had called for them; with Him; to be with

May Seventh

Talking to myself, doesn't help, as it's a
self-fulfilling prophecy
Honestly I thought that I would be thoughtfully
putting it all at ease
But the truth I don't pursue is a view that I used to
think was a type of disease
Letting it be, disengaged in the speech, as only God can
provide the mind with the peace that I seek

May Eighth

As the maybes become goodbyes
The tide continues to churn and turn
Why oh why do I allow myself to try?
I suppose it's a hold that fills to the brim inside
But I have to accept that empty pieces don't work
As I fill, I still feel, I need to "get by"
So what is it I lack, that I need to find?
Maybe my pain isn't what actually hurts
Instead it's a reaction to what I continue to deny
Yes, my faith over time has wavered
But I know that with God's favor and my commitment to His labor
My life can change; yes; turn the tide

May Ninth

Tree branches and vines dance in divine
As they wind around, upward to skies
I scream "I'm alive", as God does provide
Yes indeed; God does provide

May Tenth

This dirt road has hurt so many times, I'm beginning
to find it to be a friend
I wish I could know why, I must confide, in the fact
that I'm last once again
But as I go to the hope, that there's a cloud that floats,
waiting to take me away
I realize life is what I decide to make it, and take the
step to kneel down to God and pray

May Eleventh

The flickering of lights
Signal a new age of dance
My thoughts are my thoughts drifting dim
I have decided my life
Is at the bottom without a chance
I've prayed and I've prayed but cannot win
So why do my eyes
Glow at a glance
I've piqued; incomplete; the end
But reality sets sight
As my eyes see the light
In Christ, I am right; let's begin

J. Luke McClellan

May Twelfth

The smashing of parts
I'm defeated, defunct
My ire desires to contort
Call it evolving art
I lived through it before once
But not again, will I anymore
And I refuse for evil to start
Overtaking my trust
As I seek to complete what's in store
God lives in the stars
And is the divinity I touch
As only He can defeat satan's force

May Thirteenth

I drill into the cranium of life
Searching and working to find
The treasure of earth in a dusty, rusty old chest
As I think, I blink the lashes of my eyes
And hope that tonight
Will be the night I find the surprise that I just hopefully said
But let me be clear to reemphasize
This won't be the only time
I decide these searches won't truly address
The emptiness that lives within
Not a box but instead my own heart's den
As only God can fulfill what I expect

May Fourteenth

Buttons get pressed
And nothing to expect
But something that I couldn't see clearly
I wander to the left
And circle back to the rest
As I miss those we lost oh so dearly
And now I'm back around
To finding out just how
I wasn't quite right when I was steering
But I know the bumpy roads
I travel, I've no control
As God is who decides as I fear He

May Fifteenth

God's light is shining down
And I know that He's proud
As I'm pulled to the wool of His warmth
I see what He thinks
As He creates so much peace
In me, my heart beats; again born

J. Luke McClellan

May Sixteenth

I recognize the fuel for which has kept me going
Is addiction, not rooted in divinity
I used to be complete when my mother first had me
But since then the sin has run aplenty
And so I suppose the trouble I know
Is deeper than an ether-like sleep
So I'm making today, a new stand to say
I'm alive, well and ready, to Christ-seek

May Seventeenth

This dusk is calming
But my thoughts are spawning
New visions of anxiety amuck
And with the pain so haunting
I know I'm left wanting
Yet, only God and Christ can provide enough

J. Luke McClellan

May Eighteenth

My closet is full
Of demons for which pull
Tug and grip me ever so tightly
satans contract is annulled
As his sharpened blades dull
When God's light shines ever so brightly

May Nineteenth

Life can be so hard
When I feel I'm not enough
Or maybe it's not enough for me
Either way, here we are
Wishing what is simply wasn't
But in God, my peace is a discovery

J. Luke McClellan

May Twentieth

Yes, I can be at ease when I seek Christ
Yes, I can achieve my dreams when I speak of divine
No, I will not fold to the hold this life supplies
Yes, I only need God and Christ as my helpline

May Twenty-First

The sound of water
Rushing over rocks
Creates such a stir within
The towns by which
I feel I am lost
Are the backdrop of laurels; I pretend
I negate and reject
All of the ways of my past
But this isn't how I thought my time would end
I accept the sun's rays
As God's divine light
Yes today, in Christ, I begin

J. Luke McClellan

May Twenty-Second

We as humans
Seek to compete
Building a dynasty of sorts
It's all about the trouble
We go to in order
To accomplish this and so much more
So what is in store
For a weakened support
A species defined by success
There's only one way
To escape these ways
In Christ, we are at our very best

May Twenty-Third

Where do we place our faith in days?
Where is all our time spent?
What are the things we seek by name?
How can we survive all of this?
No one can answer, except that it's God
The knower and dreamer of good
So forget worldly thoughts and remember who brought
Salvation, as God said Christ would

J. Luke McClellan

May Twenty-Fourth

※

The genesis of our descent was invented in sin
Yes, our species is inherently flawed
The fact we retract is the math we pretend
Isn't the computation we sought
Yes we are diseased in all that we seek
Except when we go and seek God
As He is complete in the sense that we need
Everything from heartbeat to thought

※

May Twenty-Fifth

This headache of mine is taking it's time
I didn't ask to feel so much pain
It's more than the membranes, extended from mind
It's the evil that my life has portrayed
So I drink from the water that was turned into wine
And accept that Christ is God in name
Yes, He's my everything, I cherish; Divine
He is my salvation; God's way

J. Luke McClellan

May Twenty-Sixth

The spirit of my love is the nearest I have come
Washing away all of these tears
I know that I give and forgive, but not enough
As I feel that a new reckoning is near
So what's left for me in this desolate land of sand;
former sea
These beads of ocean are afar
So I think and I seek and beneath my mind's reach
God is at the center of my heart

May Twenty-Seventh

It's my chance to glow, and enhance my flow
On a roll with what I know about God
And if that is so, I can give this a go
On a roll with what I know about God

J. Luke McClellan

May Twenty-Eighth

My heart's still beating
But the blood rushing is rusty
It's metal; shards; scraps and fragments
Unequivocally I am feeding
This defeat I've been speaking
No, I don't suppose I should have this
But the reality is setting in
As I've undoubtedly been living in sin
I know I can always go right back at it
But I still choose to use
The truth I pursue in my views
As God and Christ are my pacifists

May Twenty-Ninth

Just another second to replace my ways
Just another second to erase all my shame
Just another second to debate in His name
Just another second to make Christ the reason I change

May Thirtieth

I see the opportunity
At the present; a gift
Consider it a lifetime goal achieved
Know that it isn't
What it was thought to be; descent
Into darkness, so far from it, as could be
And I realize
That time is a lie
It's nothing more than a bargaining plea
To be at ease
With all the things in this life
But only God can provide what we seek

May Thirty-First

Things beyond this existence
Defy our comprehension
As our interactions are reactions in life
The debate remains who did or didn't
Isn't worth a mention
As the fact is God is the author of our time

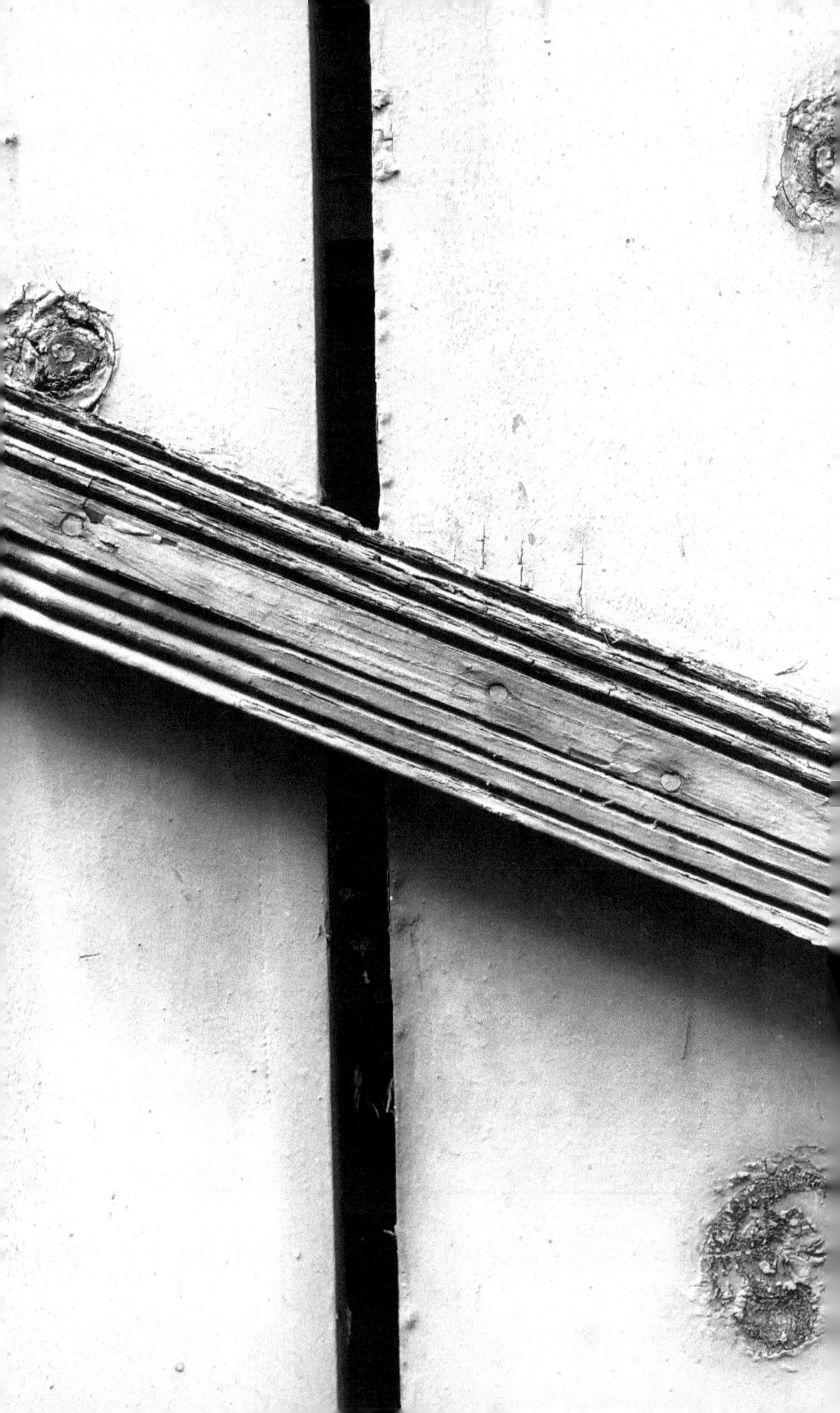

June First

Why would we try to deny ourselves
The joy that fulfills without end?
What good does it do to push and to prove
It's something else; such folly; we pretend
Purporting to know but surely you don't
But now you can find out my friend
That a life in Christ exceeds being satisfied
Supremely un-defeating defense

J. Luke McClellan

June Second

It's such a rocky hill ahead
And I know that I won't get
Anywhere when I start to make the climb
Sometimes wishing I were dead
Feeling as though nothing's left
But that's the life I've lived without Christ
So when I heard the other day
I could find another way
I thought the words were simply empty lies
But the truth that I could use
Is the honesty that God had sent us to
The fact that for us Jesus Christ had died

June Third

There's truth in my struggles
As life can seem incredulously complex
And I'm feeling that I'm out of my own breath
Such a simple way to double
Down on the sounds of my mind; perplexed
As I moan and groan aloud "I'm a wreck"
But there has to be something more
Than what I'm seeing at my front door
The teams of people speaking, cloud my mind
And I think what I'm looking for
Isn't a piece of this life's allure
It's the sign that I can align with God and Christ

J. Luke McClellan

June Fourth

〜

Maybe the ways of the saved can be me
Maybe I can take the examples and lead
Maybe I can drop to my knees; concede
Christ is the everything, I'll ever need

〜

June Fifth

My frustration is growing, festering, a downward spiral
Defeated; so I'm seeking a new hope
The equation is frankly making me insane;
it's outwardly viral
Wishing I could become solely, lone
But my refusal to succumb to the abuse of old and new
Is the initiative of a forgiving rhythm
God and Jesus, heard me from the moment
I said it to be true
My heart desires Their Divinity; free from sin

J. Luke McClellan

June Sixth

So much peace within me to unleash
I want to share this cheer; shout for joy
I see truthful ways do create a new link
A way for me to say that I've destroyed
The pain that was plain in the eyes of the beast
The monster I once used to employ
But I know that my home is the road back to He
As all evil, in this world, I avoid

June Seventh

I sing in this beautiful swing of life
But it's not my time tonight
And while it's not my time to ignite
This is my life that God surely lights
He helped me see His sight
He guides me back to what's right

J. Luke McClellan

June Eighth

I distance myself from those who need help
They clearly are not aligned with me
They think that they know but they don't and they dwell
Despising, denying what they will not see
But I feel and I heal and conceal something else
What more could there possibly be?
The hope that I won't, I change it to "will"
As God wants me to share my belief

June Ninth

I'm finding my skin flaking
As I'm shedding layers down to muscle
Hollow bone but heart veins do still pump
I'm hesitating waiting
Metamorphosis is taking
Too long for me to become strong enough
So I will end all this debating
As I begin praying
To God and Christ that my life has lost its strut
And through them, my human parts depart
Lose or win, it's life; conflicting art
I'm at ease and complete in their touch

J. Luke McClellan

June Tenth

My bitterness raged
I took back my kindness
I felt I was awakened
But I see now I was blinded
Some of them may say
What I did then was divisive
But the truth is I was in pain
And now turn to God to decry it

June Eleventh

I tend to worry when I'm lacking in faith
So why am I pacing the floor?
I know that I've hurried to correct all my ways
But still I find that I need more
So who could renew my brain's point of view
Of what I tried to provide once before?
God is the house that protects and rejects
The evil outside of its doors

J. Luke McClellan

June Twelfth

My senses don't fail me
As I give in to my needs
Wishing I could be someone else
The fact that I'm helping
Drive all possibilities
I wind up still needing more help
So I dig deep below surfaces
To find out a new way
Yet, violence is a part of my core
A fountain springs, then assures this is
Something new starting today
As God has been found here, many times before

June Thirteenth

Matters that matter aren't worthy of time
May you see this as it isn't alive
What truly assuredly will always make the difference;
thus find
God is the truth refuting the world's lies

J. Luke McClellan

June Fourteenth

A society rooted in vanity
There must be more to seek
We think we've completed the complexity
Only to find the foundation to be weak
And as the floor caves in perplexingly
It's so obvious to you and to me
That the vaccine we refuse is the inoculation we could use
God is what heals our disease

June Fifteenth

My expectations have become my downfall
As no one seems to hear my voice
I talk and I text and I convey what I expect
But to them, my words are just noise
So what can I do when I've nothing else to use
But a mind that knows how things should be?
Seek God out, as He ends the drought
And floods me with the love that I need

J. Luke McClellan

June Sixteenth

My journey in this land has been lush with demands
The people all depend upon me
They hate and they take and make me repay
For things for which I once could not see
And so I'm on knees to God praying "please"
Begging Him to guide me away
From the sin of this society but I don't need to come crying
As He always hears and listens when I pray

June Seventeenth

I have self-destructive tendencies
Where the repercussions construct enemies
My thinking is reasoning my pain
But when I touch my inner trust in He
My rush of distrust becomes a fleeting thing
And I repair the despair of my guilt and shame

J. Luke McClellan

June Eighteenth

―

I can feel God's warmth from the sun to the earth
He's in everything I touch, see and feel
I know His course is the one thing I yearn
To complete in my thoughts and prayers when I kneel

―

June Nineteenth

No job is too lofty for God
He is my strength when I am weak
Every dream conceived; believed in thought
Through Him, can be achieved

June Twentieth

I fear that my good years have drifted on by
Why must I die all alone
Feelings unknown, my isolation, cold like ice
Yet I feel I won't survive this new home
So where may I turn to when the words of discouragement ensue
Maybe it's time for me to remain unknown
The world may have faded but my faith is how I'll make it
In God as my way from those tones

June Twenty-First

This sickness is sinister, evil at best
I wish I could reverse what I did
I didn't mean to contract it but I know God protects
I am healed as I receive His gracious gift

J. Luke McClellan

June Twenty-Second

I veered from the path that God had mapped out
I feel that He's upset with my ways
But I know that I have to get back to just how
I used to be on track in His name

June Twenty-Third

A kindness in heart will always make God smile
He wants us to impart good deeds in His name
Forgive and forget and live to be with
His Agape Love in the ways we engage

J. Luke McClellan

June Twenty-Fourth

My time has come to recede the divide
The lies that have intervened in my life
I am one, with Jesus the Christ
For I am saved and He is the reason why

June Twenty-Fifth

My mission in livin' is to self-serve my vision
What else, would I help, more than me?
I think and I lead and concede I am missin'
Something I can't express but my mind believes
There's galore to this store as I stock 'till I pop
I've got more than I could possibly need
And the one way that I lack, is my faith in divine acts
But God, has touched my tender heart, to now see

June Twenty-Sixth

This is my taste, I love how it creates
Making me feel things I've never felt
The power, the fame, all tie in to play
An audition for the next step of what sells
But I fear that it's my soul, in the grip of fate
Could satan be working to help?
In this confession to self, I ask God, for me to be dealt
My shield of His divine love; make me well

June Twenty-Seventh

Three more decisions, I'm envisioning love
No one understands all this pain
In earthly terms, the depth of it hurts so much
I wish I could make it all fade
So I say this to take it as a literal stake
Truly I am slipping away
But while my faith did abate, I can renew His truth to appreciate
As I reclaim God as my change

J. Luke McClellan

June Twenty-Eighth

People will unreasonably prey on the weak
It's a sick way that takes place but it's true
I think before I speak as I dish out this peace
God has shown me indeed, how to use
The gifts by which He instilled, this is real
Life has been torment and abuse
So I'm passing it along, tell all, sing in song
Let's put God in our minds; faith renewed

Devotional Rhyme

June Twenty-Ninth

I never met someone that I didn't love
As people are a creation of God
But I'm thoughtfully honestly expressing I don't like
Most as they don't align at all
With the way I think as I pray just to be
The best person I can possibly be
Wishing for more, then God checks me at the door
As He reminds me I sin with the rest of humanity

J. Luke McClellan

June Thirtieth

The glow of the moon
Is showing fine through
The light of the night is divine
I feel God's presence
As He's arranged purely Heaven-sent
Things just for me that shine bright

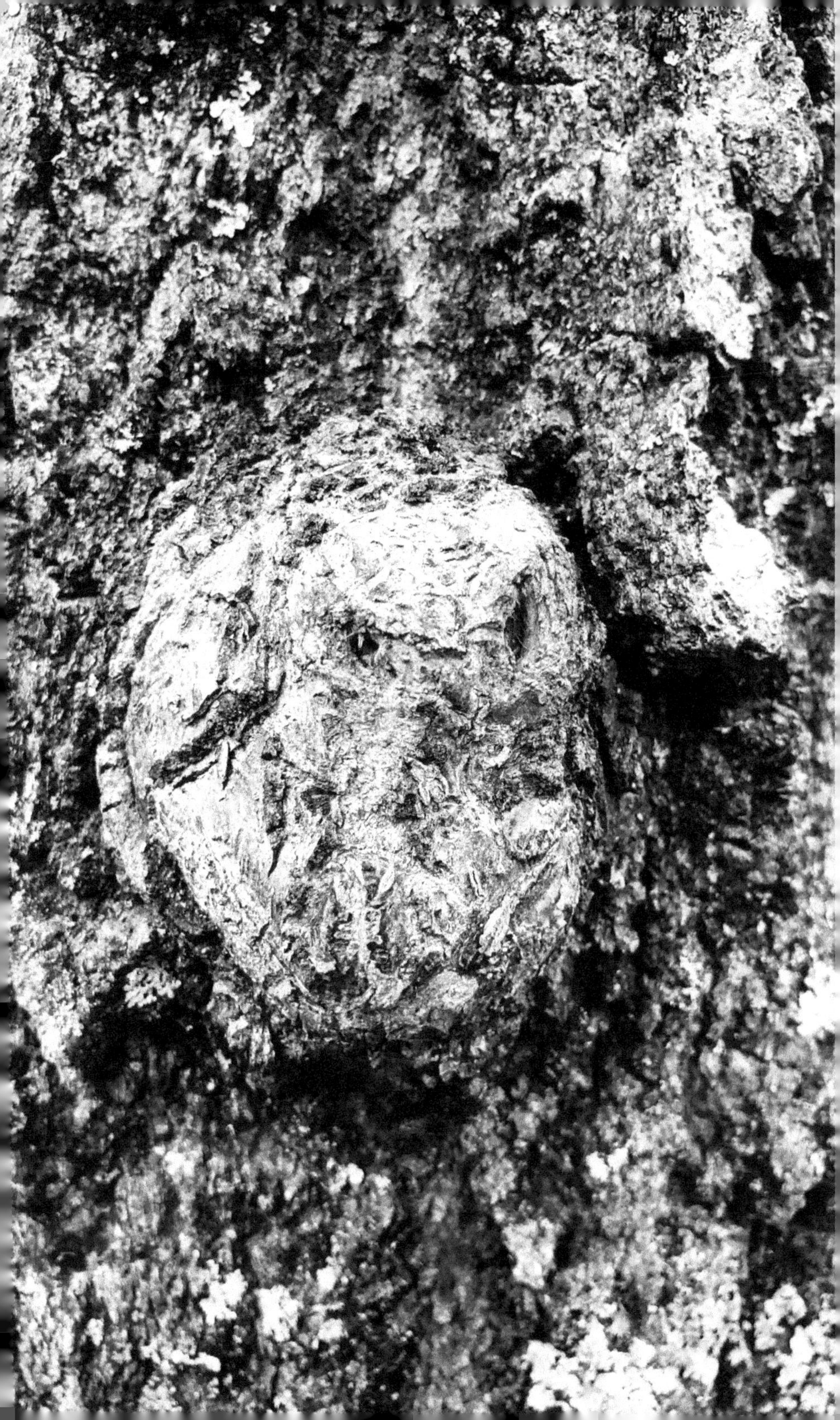

J. Luke McClellan

July First

I've concluded the news is
To stay true to the truth
That "Truth" being that Jesus is King
So do not hate on the ways
That God set forth for our days
It is He; never we; no debating

July Second

He moves me like the moon, will do with the currents
Shaking their space; an earthquake
He's impossible to refuse and I expect this occurrence
To be the very reason it hurts to say
"Please don't ever leave, you are the way I believe,
I'm renewed in You as a human being."
But God knows and He thinks, anticipating;
holding the key
And for this, I am whisked away; unseen

J. Luke McClellan

July Third

Subversive thoughts do work to get you lost
Forget all your troubles and be still
God is The Rock as His Kingdom is sought
For your patience, one day, will be revealed

Devotional Rhyme

July Fourth

I have a new face; ugly paint
And I destroy all the cracks emitting light
Don't ask for the way; no complaints
God has now given me His divine sight

J. Luke McClellan

July Fifth

Believing what I deserve
Is my earned downfall
As the rocks that I climb disintegrate
My peace within me is only heard
When I call
Up to God for His help for my escape
But I know that I'll serve
My own fate when I face
The discomfort of my ambivalent ways
Peace is restored on the earth
As I bring to knees, my all
God in my heart indeed, is awake

July Sixth

The clothes that I am wearing
Are the mold that I am carrying
I am cold when I'm told to obey
I sold my soul, so very
Unknown why I am tearing
My life to disparaging, damaging shame
So I deform my form of caring
And bury the essence of cherishing
And construct a new way from this dusty clay
As I seek to embody Christ's sharing
The principles by which He married
And made them the identity of His divine way

J. Luke McClellan

July Seventh

I'm fenced in to this offensive sin
I'm in the den by which I choose
I do what I do in an effort to live
But my view is I'm already doomed
So who, if it's true, can re-shape and bend
The ways I've decided to use
Not you, not me, only Jesus can give
Salvation to be accepted within as Truth

July Eighth

The lights in the sky illuminate the clouds
Setting atmospheric currents that divulge
The sweetest pleasantries that we could possibly allow
And yet there seems to be something unknown
For that it is artistic freedom I demand
No, I cannot stand to be contained
Yet, there's more to this life than we will ever understand
As God is our constant; unchanged

July Ninth

Door handles and windows
Tires on cars
All provide purpose we see
Mechanisms affect rhythms we know
From afar
And yet gaps remain for which we cannot speak
So, the perplexing Earth works fast and slow
A pulsating heart
The life-force dancing in the streets
Yet God is the grand architect
Of this universe of art
Achieving what we cannot process to believe

July Tenth

The city shines in the bright light; divine
Only God could provide such beauty
And the meaning is a sight that's purely sublime;
Oh my, what a picture to envy
And this is a missed opportunity of kinds
That binds our minds to plenty
But the fact remains, God never will change
He is our fulfillment when empty

J. Luke McClellan

July Eleventh

Hollow points with a jagged edge
Cut so deep into flesh
The decay that's in place, here instead
Is what we think is for the best
But the idea we evade, Christ as Head
What else could we expect?
We lack in the peace that God has said
We'd achieve if we believed He protects

July Twelfth

Balloons in the sky, floating to space
Capturing clouds along paths
Never to decide, just where to remain
Yet somehow find their way back
Descending in time, never to take
A new place when they retract
Yet the simplest things, unequivocally
God made in creation; it's fact

J. LUKE McCLELLAN

July Thirteenth

When giants overtake and replace
What you knew
When the mightiest forsake the love
Thought to be true
Never doubt again
As this moment is you
God is your friend
The one constant; He proves

July Fourteenth

I thought I knew everything
And yet I'm devoid of knowledge
I thought I could really be
The one to overcome and abolish
The pain inside my brain, see
It's an emptiness I have thought with
But only in God, do I really think
Clearly, I'm at peace; let's call it

J. Luke McClellan

July Fifteenth

My riches are given from God up above
No one else could provide
Never have I been with a new sense of love
Indeed through He and Christ, I'm alive

July Sixteenth

My fear overcomes when I'm one with God
My taboos are my views; defunct
My pride too then dies when I confide in all
Christ, the Divine, for me does

J. Luke McClellan

July Seventeenth

The lights shine down on an empty field
I'm the only player that's here to risk
It's my life tonight and I'm alive; so real
As I need a savior for me to be here with
And I look up above and see the lights down
Blinding my eyes as they shine
I'm benign in my life in attempts to be crowned
Only Christ is the King and He's mine

July Eighteenth

Jupiter blues from the Earth to the Moon
I'm not used to a mood with this tune
Brain chemicals; doomed; insane, but it's true
Incorrect; you can rest in God's Truth

J. Luke McClellan

July Nineteenth

My mindset is ripe with regret I guess
I'm alive but I'm tired of no change
I wish I could take out a tire-iron to inspect
The flat feeling in my mind, that remains
So how do I inflate my ways and go get
My life to stop remaining the same
Direct back to God and He'll correct all these thoughts
I am healed and unbound in His name

July Twentieth

The ripples in water are echoing my thoughts
Billows of force unnoticed
I see though life's harder as I'm seemingly lost
Wishing someone else here could know it
But how do I spark a new truth, evoking renewed
Feelings of luxurious style and weight
The pressure I've fallen prey to as only God knew
He would be my new path taken today

J. Luke McClellan

July Twenty-First

Our immaturities are surely heard and seen
There isn't a worthy note to be noted; so it seems
Unless we can pray on knees today and sing
God is the greatest who made us and Christ is King

July Twenty-Second

I pray for this pain to end on this day
As my heart is stricken with so much grief
I miss my beloved; but have changed my ways
As God resides in how I wish to be

July Twenty-Third

This lonely heart of mine is only going to be fine
When I confide in the love that God gives
This lonely heart of mine is only going to be fine
When I recognize Christ died, so I could live

July Twenty-Fourth

I've figured out that my doubt is somehow vanquished
When I'm at peace being in Christ
I've decided I'm biding my time for right now; enchanted
As I'll enter His kingdom one night

J. Luke McClellan

July Twenty-Fifth

The fountain sprays and takes a moment to correct
As the wind from the ends of Earth erupt
The closure, poignant exposure, is rough and expects
The peace that's beneath to be enough
But there's uprising in here and oh my, how it's clear
These shattered dreams do seem to be stuck
So without further ado, my friends, I present to you
God as the love to succumb

July Twenty-Sixth

These walls are enclosed and form a hollow storm
No, there won't be any free thought
It's cost is a lot but it's got to be brought
Back down to the ground; not lost
So how do these molecules connect to affect
The time that I spend to dine on collaboration
I can evade this place as my heart dissipates
For Christ is my new found salvation

J. Luke McClellan

July Twenty-Seventh

The sirens alarm and find the silent tune
Whispers diminish; adrift
Distant we hear it but it isn't to be true
As the calm wholeheartedly seems fit
And my conscience says to stay but my heart says to go
As the perils are clearly alive
My finding is timing the evident stranglehold
Relinquishing this midnight storm in Christ

July Twenty-Eighth

No further explanation is needed
No wandering from land to sea
No settlement has come before and depleted
My pondering, shaking legs' knees
And my rattling bones may be battling alone
But the truth isn't what I did think
As God and Jesus, I now seeketh at all times
From the womb to the grave they're with me

J. Luke McClellan

July Twenty-Ninth

God is my peace when I fall down to pieces
Jesus is within reach, as I pick them back up
God to me speaks, when I fly high undefeated
As Jesus calls me back down; my feet touch

July Thirtieth

❦

This day I am miserable, literally in pain
My heart beats but my mind is still
Experiencing temperamental thoughts in the brain
But I seek, I am lost, I am ill
So wishing to abate the ways of this malaise
I don't know how else to be healed
But I find deep inside as I pray up to Christ
My woes go subside, as revealed

❦

J. Luke McClellan

July Thirty-First

I am thankful for the greatness
God has bestowed upon me
He's made me see I need to lead
I am grateful to be anxious
As my pain is relating
Connecting people to God, with ease

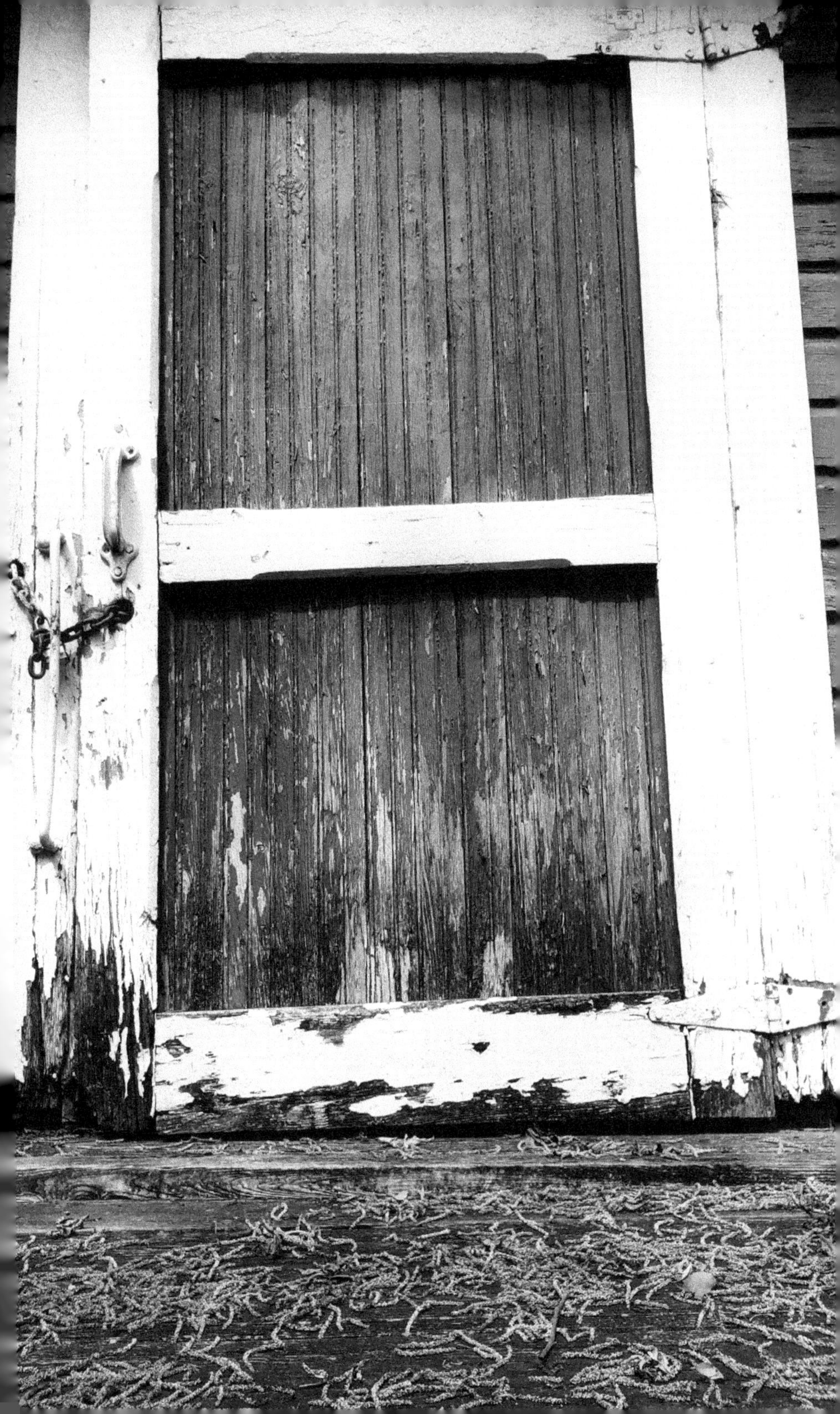

J. Luke McClellan

August First

When we travel about
Wishing to get out
A heart stops to share in the pain
Let them know how
You are healed now
As God is why peace has been gained

August Second

We all wish we could invent a new trick
A way to take away fear
But there's no such thing as it doesn't exist
As God is the reckoning that's clear

August Third

Life can be discouraging as this world beats you down
Dragging you along in the mire
But don't allow those words to hollow your heart out
You too can give back, to inspire
Let them all know that there is a safer road
And it begins and ends in Christ
That journey isn't alone as it's one to behold
Your salvation is the only way to get by

August Fourth

The mood is somber and my thoughts drift to pain
Why must life be this way?
I feel it's an honor to have crossed paths on this day
But I've decided I can no longer stay
So allow me the opportunity to be at peace with us
As we inevitably delay
The rift that rips, circumventing our trust
Only God can heal our shame

J. Luke McClellan

August Fifth

The darkest corners of the earth are bordering our hurt
We focus and hope that it's done
But in order to restore back the path of our work
We must first trust in God's only Begotten Son

August Sixth

The calmness and still of the moment is clear
The items I loved are now lost
The settled simplicity of the night disappears
For this life is not what I once thought
And as I divide commitments and time
I know I'm so cold to be thawed
As only the warmth of God, like a storm's lightning rod
Brings me to my knees as I'm called

J. Luke McClellan

August Seventh

The sunset's glow begets the unknown
As I marry the very sentiment
I was meant to be alone in He, I do own
My life as a prize serving Him in it

August Eighth

This is my time to resign from this life
The ways of the depraved and the ill
As I'm guilty of plenty mistakes; can't deny
But I'm perfect in serving Christ's will

J. Luke McClellan

August Ninth

The pressure that's building erupts in my head
This feeling is crushing my skull
I accept the essence that I am defeated; dead
But I've a spark of resilience that I pull
From my heart that is hardened and starting to get full
Of the regret and pain from what was said
But behold I know that only God can annul
As He, through Christ, I accept

August Tenth

I am feeling relief, I thank God that He
Provides the peace that I need
God is my light, Holy Star so bright
Divinely arranged, I believe

J. Luke McClellan

August Eleventh

Finding my way in the darkness of night
There's no brightness or light; it's devoid
I'm hopeful but won't go down tunnels without sight
It's clearly appearing to be a ploy
Introspectively speaking as I'm met with these feelings
Descending down roads of self-loathing and acts
The layers of my skin begin to start peeling;
thoughts uneasy
But with God I can create divine paths

August Twelfth

Trust in God; ignore your thoughts
Pay no mind to your brain
Trust in God; ignore your thoughts
In Christ, the Divine, you are changed

J. Luke McClellan

August Thirteenth

My dreams aren't for me
As they need to serve God
I'm lost at what cost but know what I've got
He believes in me
To fulfill my belief
Spreading His word, to be heard by all

August Fourteenth

Holes in this earth are hurting the worth
I seek but I think I'm beneath
The land I command as I stand to work
For God is the meaning I need

J. Luke McClellan

August Fifteenth

I'm feeling disgraced, as I pace this place
The doors are locked and I'm stuck
Wishing I was given a new way to replace
The conundrum that has run amuck
So what is left for me to believe in these things
I've never felt safe, to here stay
This life is bereft; I could die, I'm so vexed
But Christ is the hope that remains

August Sixteenth

Only God can determine our value and worth when
We submit to the gift that He brought
The value of Christ knowing for us He died then
We are saved in accepting this cost

J. Luke McClellan

August Seventeenth

My soul is the element for the Kingdom of God
As Jesus is the Key to enter
No longer in my thoughts, will my peace be robbed
I confess I've digressed as a sinner
As the freedom I seek is deep inside me
Knowing good and well I am saved
The dawn will arrive as I know I confide
In the light of the Christ as I pray

August Eighteenth

Streetlights seem bright when I look up to skies
My head spins with west winds; alas
But the calm comes along, singing songs of the Christ
Jesus is the peace that will last

J. Luke McClellan

August Nineteenth

The mistakes I've made
Are plain to see
My conscience is the Holy Spirt alive
Why I decide to play
And willingly go cheat
Is beyond me as I sit here to deny
But wishing I could save
Myself from the things
Which threaten to destroy my life
It's true, I'm okay
When I'm willing to be
One with God and the Christ

August Twentieth

The peace Christ provides in my need to be alive
It's organic and naturally calm
I would never divide, myself from His side
Jesus heals my weakness; I am strong

J. Luke McClellan

August Twenty-First

All my broken parts
Are tokens torn from my heart
Coins of exploited, demonic pain
But beneath the disease I breathe
I believe I am a part
And one with Christ in His name

August Twenty-Second

It's the interpreting of thoughts
That leads to anxiety
And creates the misery we live
But in accepting what the mind caught
And simply letting it ride free
The remainder is the peace Christ is

J. Luke McClellan

August Twenty-Third

I realize I obsess
Over the digression of my mind
My thoughts retain all control
But despite my regret
Wishing there was something else to find
God soothes; Jesus heals, these mental woes

August Twenty-Fourth

Self-talk
Is the dwelling spot
Misery festers and builds
To be free from these thoughts
Receiving peace at no cost
Confide in Christ as your will

J. Luke McClellan

August Twenty-Fifth

The unfulfilling road
That is still being told
Is a journey that certainly ends
But when we join in His hope
As our lives unfold
It's a destiny to gloriously begin

August Twenty-Sixth

My heart beat is slow; then stops in my movement
As I never sit still in my mind
My body deceives as I think I can do it
But the truth is I'm used by my lies
So how do I find the my life to be renewed
As I think and I speak I am fine
But that is not truth as only God can change views
And imbue the peace He designed

J. Luke McClellan

August Twenty-Seventh

The ceiling my head hits is the feeling I'm met with
The throbbing is the flow of my blood
Symbolically speaking, I'm calling all good things
To help ease the pain that's too much
I continue then waiting for my new troubles to begin fading
As such, I have not much luck
Oh, no more debating, I'm tired of this aching
God is the aid I can trust

Devotional Rhyme

August Twenty-Eighth

⁓

If I consider an extension from the present I'm in
I simply get really overwhelmed
And if I ponder how much harder life might be again
When "things" come back, creating hell
I need to need recede and retreat to the basics
As He understands what I tell
I think and I do, but should stop for the Truth
God and Christ; my peace where I dwell

⁓

J. Luke McClellan

August Twenty-Ninth

Sometimes the addiction seems too strong to hold
It's a force that is powerful; I submit
The truth of the matter is, it's satan as the unknown
He's destroying my life to pieces and bits
So how can I overcome, what "eases" my woes
I'm a slave to the ways of "this"
God is the "known" to defeat the devil's lies
Christ, my friends is what's "it"

Devotional Rhyme

August Thirtieth

Seeking validation, from invalid information
Is a waste of time, to give
Seek Him as your way, when you feel this temptation
As in He, is the way to live

J. Luke McClellan

August Thirty-First

I'm tired of fighting this battle
The life of addiction and pain
Maybe it's my time to rattle
This coffin of mine from the grave
As I see the simple "how though's?"
As a means for me to stay the same
The Holy Spirit is devout and flows
As in Christ, I know I can change

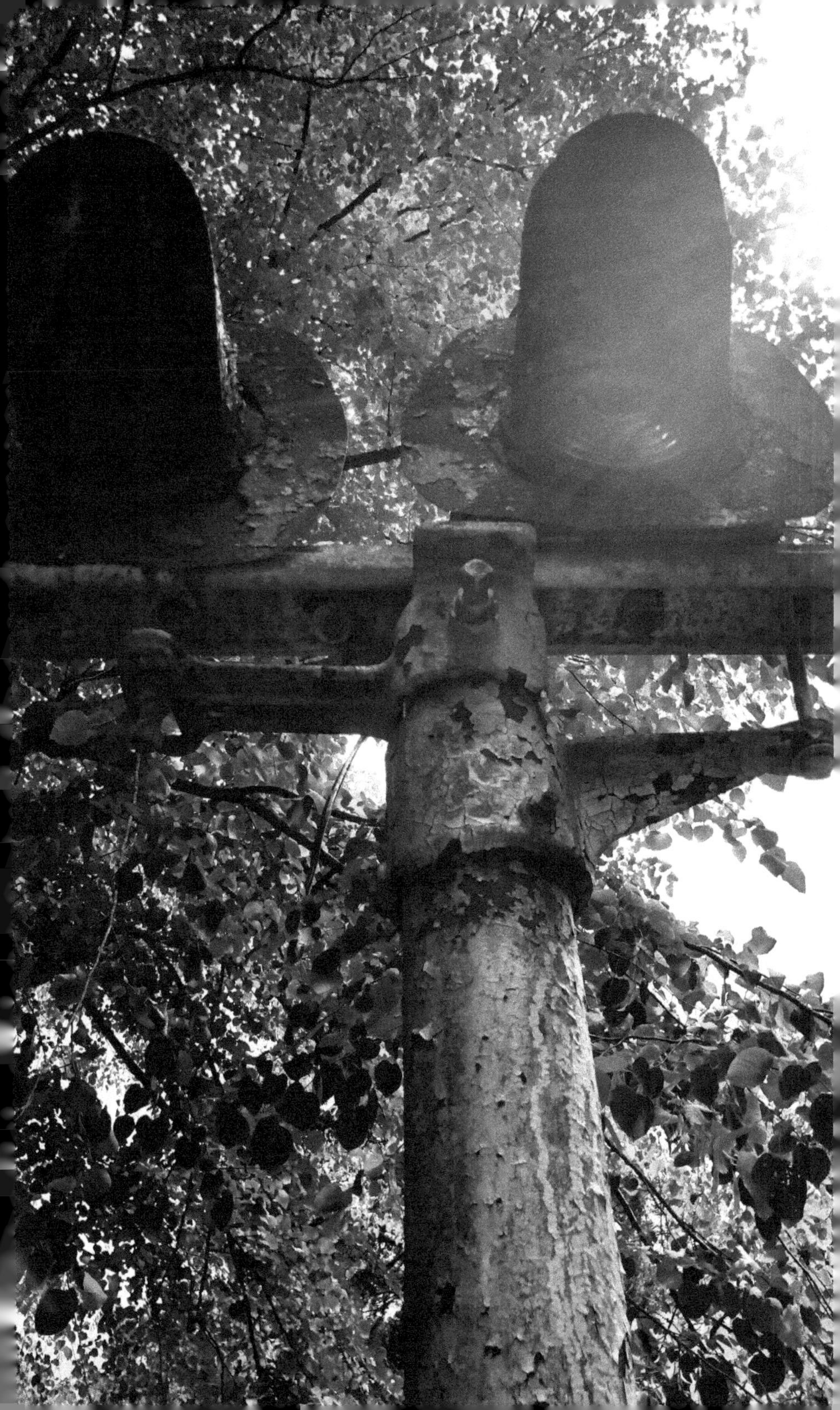

J. Luke McClellan

September First

I feel I've lost the motivation
To keep on and on like expected
The cost has been so agitatin'
As my heart feels defeated and rejected
So how can I say when to stop this rotation
Of pain, denial and no protection
And that's when Christ heard, what I just said
And provides me with life that's worth waitin'

September Second

I can't find happiness, not even peace
Why would I want to press forward?
I'm mad at this reality, that the problem is me
So what more can I do, what more?
It's a harrowing feeling of guilt and defeat
So why would I want to press forward?
Digging deep down more deeply, I believe I'll find plenty
The love of God and Christ is the "what more".

September Third

The good times that shine are designed by divine
Yes, God is the center of illumination
And the shame in crimes and commitment of lies
Are designed by the evil ways of satan
So just sit by on stand-by, and ride out the waves
God's ways will always go back to Creation
He designed this Earth to work peacefully each day
As He sent Jesus Christ; our salvation

September Fourth

I continue to use and abuse the view
It's okay to behave with self-love
But the truth in this news is the way that we do
Self-indulging and exploiting; not enough
So we like to go reach and think we complete
When achieving the next XYZ thing
But God wants us to seek Him, not ourselves to depend
He provides for our lives what we need

J. Luke McClellan

September Fifth

The demons in life are beneath our own lies
They lurk and they prey on our sin
It's the essence of satan in the flesh, just disguised
As he believes, that we, are all friends
So don't be deceived; underneath all the highs
The lows, will only grow, deep within
Follow the peace, all for which, Christ preached
God is the light in this den

September Sixth

My mind is bruised from the times I've been used
I never thought this world could be so cruel
Until I started living, people's nature; unforgiving
And now I simply think I'm a fool
As I have been wishing, for a life that's pretending
To be something I have not ruled
But then God reached down to me, and from Him, I heard speak
"Bring others to me, this, you must do."

J. Luke McClellan

September Seventh

◦∞◦

My struggles are evident
As I'm met with such affliction
I get that I'm sick in my heart
But God has taught me this
That there is no good reason
Trust in He, and we will never, be apart

◦∞◦

September Eighth

The sun is erupting from behind the dark clouds
It's been there; calm; dormant, still
It's the one thing that is divine but no talk of is allowed
Everywhere, all of the light spills
It's true that the view of Him has been diminished
Reduced to a life-force that's been killed
But the good news here is, God is alive and convinced
We're worth sparing, yes, our God is real

J. Luke McClellan

September Ninth

What's that falling from the clouds in the sky?
It's an undefined substance; unclear
It's not precipitation or any kind of changing
Weather that never appears
It seems to be suiting that we find it to be ruining
The ways that are paved up ahead; near
No, it's God the Divine, that's felt after each storm's time
Jesus, we have much faith, in you here

Devotional Rhyme

September Tenth

A weakened mind-state has become my mistake
I'm frozen and know when to stop
I'm holding onto things that I should simply let be
As I decide, to my knees, I will drop
"God, please hear me, I love you so dearly
I know where to go when I'm lost
You are my solace; the calmest, simply honest
The peace, I do need, which I've now got

J. Luke McClellan

September Eleventh

I've cleared out my mind for the sake of time
Who knows how much we have left
It's evident in the way that I make these words rhyme
But I'd rather not spend it perplexed
As the love God gives, is the purest experience
We will ever, possibly achieve
Forgiving, understanding, undemanding, aplenty
Jesus, I need this, I believe

September Twelfth

My doubt has left me feeling weary and tired
Wishing I could be inventing something new
An emotion allowed out; not so concealing with self-ire
So how can I possibly escape this view?
I need to find within me a release of self-peace
That I can express; not vex; feeling renewed
But the truth is the only one who can do this is me
Through God and Christ, yes this, I can do

J. Luke McClellan

September Thirteenth

A state a being alone is a state I'm competing to dethrone
Yet, never a whisper can ever be heard
A disease that's known in me; shown; so ugly
And yet no one else can utter a word
So here I am sitting, sifting through these thoughts
Such a cost for always being right
But when I lower down to kneel, I then begin to feel
The light in me, provided, by Christ

September Fourteenth

The complexities of this world are affecting my head's pearls
The beauty that resides in my mind
A destructor of sorts and we've been here before
But I realize this time I am fine
As God is my hero and my tears go to roll
Streaming down my face like a river
God is the giver, the Truth here forever
The only Perfect Love that I know

September Fifteenth

I feel the sandpit is handing me its grip
My teeth grit as I think it's my demise
The grains seep in and my mind doesn't think it can win with
My heart's will alone; I've surmised
So who can I find, to take over my mundane ideas, so trite?
Afflicted with indifference and lies?
My pulse-rate increases as in the name of Jesus
God in the Flesh, I accept, for my life

September Sixteenth

The shingles to my home's roof
Have been lifted by the wind
The storm is approaching quickly; fast
And if there is a single ounce of doubt without proof
We can stop all of the pretense
And allow ourselves to quickly react
But what good would any of that do
When we are trapped down in sin
As our thoughts respond to our acts
And the reverse too is also true
And only Christ can simply end
The pain we endure, it's a fact

September Seventeenth

My Christian Faith is the precedent I choose to convey
It's the way for which God wants me to live
It's not about my needs or what more life could be
Serving He is the most fulfilling of all gifts

September Eighteenth

I've felt something new today
At the core of my heart's love
I think that my views have changed
As I dream and believe in all He does
For Jesus is the cornerstone of being saved
I accept and leave behind what was
For these are the greatest words I can say
"I submit and give Christ all my trust."

J. Luke McClellan

September Nineteenth

Listening to my heartbeat's rhythms
I'm seeking to find what I need within them
The essence of peace but it isn't just given
It's only achieved in the belief in Him

September Twentieth

A gathering of minds, succinct in time
Divine and quite fine in their love
For the truth comes out when they move their mouths
In Christ's cloth, they are cut of

J. Luke McClellan

September Twenty-First

This feast for which Jesus spoke was of love
A breaking of bread and pouring of wine
His body was given and spilled was His blood
Taking our sins for us to live eternal life

Devotional Rhyme

September Twenty-Second

The sins of our past can come up to react
With the ways we behave in our present
Not that we should activate such hate to be brash
It's just fact that life is what we make it
So it's best to create good choices and avoid bad
Yes, live today like your last, appreciate it
Feel the love of God as He dissolves all of the trash
For your peace, in Christ's name, we say it

J. Luke McClellan

September Twenty-Third

This fire within my heart
Burns for the Word of God
As Christ is inside my mind
He defines the calm when apart
From His peace that I was taught
I reclaim His name, in mine

September Twenty-Fourth

The diversity of this life
Can create suicidal strife
As feelings like these are of concern
But the truth of the matter is the way
God subdues the night
He is the peace for which we yearn

J. Luke McClellan

September Twenty-Fifth

I feel that I've emptied aplenty my soul
As only God knows what I've been through
He sees the disease for which the pain of this world brings
And on my knees, to He, I pray to

September Twenty-Sixth

Sing me a song, that the angels stay strong
Presently, benevolently, healing strife
As I know what the Word says, in Christ I'll never see death
Infinity, is He, as my life

J. Luke McClellan

September Twenty-Seventh

I feel the love as the love of God works
It's essential for the reciprocal in full
God helps, heals, tells, reveals
That in Christ, with His might, our sins are annulled

September Twenty-Eighth

The challenges I take in this life; I'm so afraid
Darkness stands tall in my eyes
I realize the size of my denial has been a shame
As the truth remains; I am indeed still alive
And when I take into account my diction and how I portray
The fact that I partake in egregious lies
I shake away the old ways and accept God as my new face
And embrace His omnipotent place in my life

J. Luke McClellan

September Twenty-Ninth

God has called me to seek out those willing
To receive His Olive Branch of Peace
He wants me to speak of Him as the Truth as it has been
The fulfillment in serving Jesus and He

September Thirtieth

Creating a stripped down, more basic life
Imagining the time as Christ came and went
How blessed we are, yet have become so far apart
From the closeness, God designed us to live

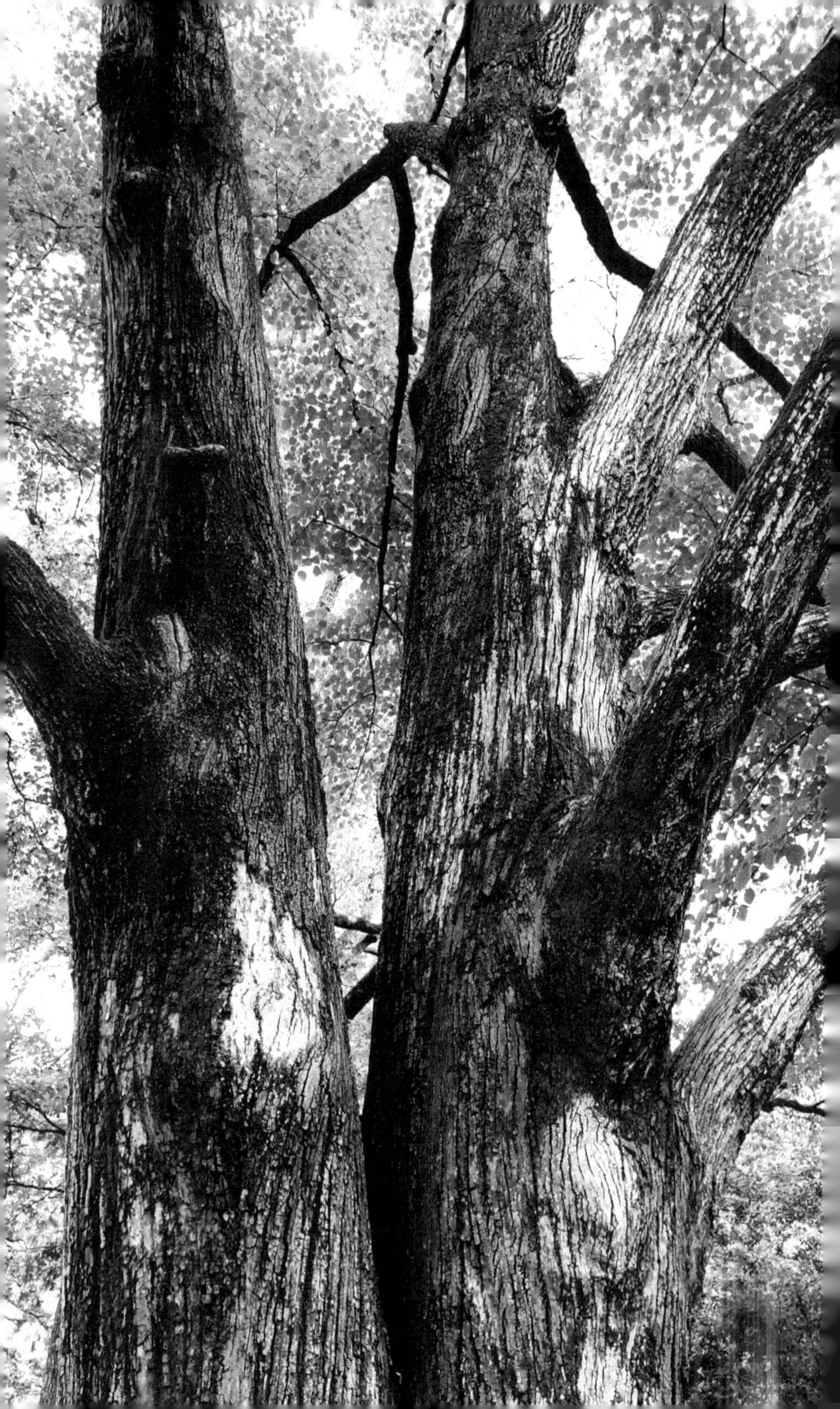

October First

Thought-provoking statements not "hoping" for change it's
Demanding, but as God wants us to do
He sees and believes and needs us to live
As close to Him and Christ, to renew
The ways which we behave and save our loving change
As the standard; a metric we accept as truth
God is our foundation, for defacing the pain when
It becomes too much to suffer the abuse

J. Luke McClellan

October Second

The places to sit
Underneath the earth's trees
Create a stirring that makes me love more
The truth is ever since
I was finally able to see
In God and Christ I found what I'm in this for
As I lived a life of shame and can't forget
I wish it hadn't been me
But I know in Jesus, I am restored
I'm relinquishing the past tense
As I choose to live my best existence
A life of God and Christ, by them, I'm adored

Devotional Rhyme

October Third

The most apparent reason
Is the one we are too blind to see
Reading; thinking; achieving
We believe that our natural seasons
Are the ways for which to lead
But we never stop to realize the true meaning
So we continue dancing along
As we hum tunes to new songs
And think "this is it" and there's no time like the present
But we simply couldn't be more wrong
As the truth was revealed at the cross
And God inspired us in Christ; His best gift

J. Luke McClellan

October Fourth

May we sing and praise the Lord today
For He raised His son from the dead
Let's celebrate and rejoice in the ways
Doing, just as He said

October Fifth

Despite the times I've sighed and cried
Wishing for something less
Despite the binds I denied were mine
Creating a much bigger mess
There is one thing, I achieved to believe
And I know much more than I guessed
Acceptance of Christ as my life to be
The moment my heartache and pain left

October Sixth

Jesus has become the quintessential solution
A resolution; affixed in my existence
Ever since then, I separated from all the noise of this world's pollution
His life then; in mine, became prominent

October Seventh

The beauty I observe in the stars above the Earth
Deserve to be recognized for their worth
From the dust in the clouds to the sounds that bellow out
This too, has value, to be observed
For it's often overlooked, all the days that it took
To create such wonderment; I'm astonished
But we need to be honest, in believing that all of this
Is a creation, of the innovation, that God is

J. Luke McClellan

October Eighth

The judgment for which I suddenly express
Isn't meant to be dealt with such scrutiny
It's meant to be met with a moment of peace, but I suspect
The ways it's perceived isn't truth in He
So I guess the best method of avoiding these tactics
Is to go back to the ways Jesus taught me
Give nothing but love, turning cheeks to succumb
It's God's job, to judge us, as it ought to be

October Ninth

Relatable pain is debatable the same
Maybe we should agree that we hurt
It's worth it to work on feeling trauma undeserved
As we stir and conjure up God's Holy Words
Yes, He is a force that came before our birth
An omnipotence we will never get or comprehend
In a matter of seconds, He could destroy us all
Yes, He is our God, amen.

J. Luke McClellan

October Tenth

The most peaceful place we think and debate
Wasting away our time
We hate and then pray and pray more, then hate
It's all moot in truth, but let's align
In the fact that the math we add or subtract
Is how we react to our lies
So let's face the ways, we've lost and starting today
Accept God and Christ in our lives

October Eleventh

I could start again and pretend
My pretense is in Jesus, but it's not
I need to shed the lies I said and I spread
And accept Christ's blood in my thoughts

J. Luke McClellan

October Twelfth

I seek Jesus as I need this in my life
But the devil knows where I live
Deflecting the infecting, evil, sinister lies
The Crown of Thorns of Christ in me; it ends

October Thirteenth

The laughter I hear from across the aisle
Is an embarrassing mockery of me
And after I veer to all of the smiles
I see all I need to see
Then think and recede in disbelief for a while
How could God allow this to be
But God didn't do it and I know what the truth is
In He, and Christ, I am set free

October Fourteenth

The trouble with living in this world is
Trust is a dying trait
But the most alarming evidence to support this
Society refuses to wait
Everything is sellable in a moment's notice
But they don't know it's hate
As when God is absent, evil relapses
But in Christ, satan's lies, will abate

October Fifteenth

Let's wash away the pain that's changed
The life we used to live
Let's talk today and pause the ways
Interactions have failed to forgive
All the mistakes, seem to take place
In cycles denying who is
King of this world, Jesus is heard
He reigns supreme; God is

J. Luke McClellan

October Sixteenth

I sense a pretentious vision
A decline in finding me attractive
The fact I've given my life to live for them
They deny my time and act like it's
Not worth theirs with me to interact with
So maybe I should find a new healthy habit
Time with Christ, no better way to live life
As He overcomes what's disastrous

October Seventeenth

God hears me when my knees are shaking
He warms me when my lips are blue
He heals me when my needs are taking
Nefarious turns and I'm confused
Though I know He wants me baking
When temperatures only rise a degree or two
He still remains patiently waiting
For me to seek Him out; the Truth

J. Luke McClellan

October Eighteenth

What holds our commitment
In a world of distractions
The sparkles, so hard to resist
It's evident we can't resist it
Putting no discipline into action
Only Christ can renew how we live

October Nineteenth

I'm missing you; where are you
Can you feel me? I'm still here
This darkness has overtaken me
The way that I felt so close to
The times we had were mere
Moments of my own reality
But though in this life you are through
I lose my eyes in tears
And this constricts my ability to speak
But God is who you're with now
As I one day will be too and oh how
I look forward, back to you, I will reach

J. Luke McClellan

October Twentieth

Humility is a quality that God wants us to seek
Arrogance has no place in His heart
He desires our commitment to be rooted in peace
As we embody Christ in who we are

October Twenty-First

God wants us to praise
And give thanks to Him
Regardless of what's happening in our lives
Whether joy or pain
Being what we live in
God is always with us, by our side

J. Luke McClellan

October Twenty-Second

The thoughts that come about, seem to shout aloud
in my head
Telling me that I'm not enough
The cost is somehow, linked to a sense of dread; I yell back:
"This anxiety, that's inside of me, is too much!"
And so what do I have left, after all is done and said
I think my reasoning should be the touch
That stops these thoughts from speaking, but the truth is
who I'm needing
Jesus; who I now seeketh; in He I trust

October Twenty-Third

The trees with leaves are blown by the wind
The calm is still present in the air
The needs of our being are known only by Him
As all will be evident in our prayers

J. Luke McClellan

October Twenty-Fourth

We can excavate this place and take our time to find
The treasures we know here exist
But we don't understand that the only true way is by
A route that's devout; but this isn't it
So we can replace our shame with something more sublime
The Kingdom of God is what's rich
Yes, let us forget, the treachery of life's script
God and Christ; the Divine; in us live

October Twenty-Fifth

I pray for everyone that's sitting on the side of a building
As I know the pain seems too great to go on
I pray for the failure that's been for them inside killing
The soul they used to know to be so strong
But the truth is there's no truer sense
Of finding a better way
When we seek out God and lay claim to His name
Jesus feels, Jesus heals, Jesus saves

J. Luke McClellan

October Twenty-Sixth

My life is a flash; an electric bolt that strikes
Decimating those who hate me
Revenge is the sweetest memory I have in my life
Only twice, but now it's time, to make it three
With such a plot to devise, nothing stopping my rise
It's the greatest sensation; animosity
But then an overtaking was felt, as my knees buckled;
I knelt
Jesus reached down, and in He, I am relieved

Devotional Rhyme

October Twenty-Seventh

The sun drops beneath
The skyline that I see
And I think and I pray and I think
Another night ahead of me
As my anxiety always likes to tease
"What if?" No, please—let me be!
But the one God thinks I truly need
Is the Prince, no "THE KING!"
Jesus, yes, you better believe
So I sit here pondering
As my mind continues wandering
Yet, "The Truth", will always set me free

J. Luke McClellan

October Twenty-Eighth

I've hit a breaking-point that I can't live with any longer
My melancholy heart aches to its core
I explore each exploit in my grief-stricken mind that ponders
And I wander off the map wishing for so much more
Oh how I adore, my time once experienced before
What was had is now eternally, forever lost
And yes, the complexities of these deceitful times have my love torn
But in Jesus, I'm relieved, of this cost

Devotional Rhyme

October Twenty-Ninth

What seems right is decidedly scorned for its truth
The truth for which Christ sets us free
And all the troubles of this secular world seclude
Our hearts from the love of God's peace
So let it be known that those attempting to hold
Us captive from our freedom of religious speech
They will never change the ways of my Christ-filled heart
As I'm forever saved; cemented in He

J. Luke McClellan

October Thirtieth

I feel God's presence in my every thought
I carry Him with me in each step of my life
This walk that I'm on isn't perplexing; never lost
As The Holy Spirit is my compass back to right

Devotional Rhyme

October Thirty-First

~~~

Some think that the way life goes is a hoax
A curse for which they're afflicted
But given the fact that we all experience bad
It isn't quite like that, now is it?
So listen for a moment to the heartbeat of your struggles
God is the presence that you need
You too can overcome the evil that hums
As He is the peace we all seek

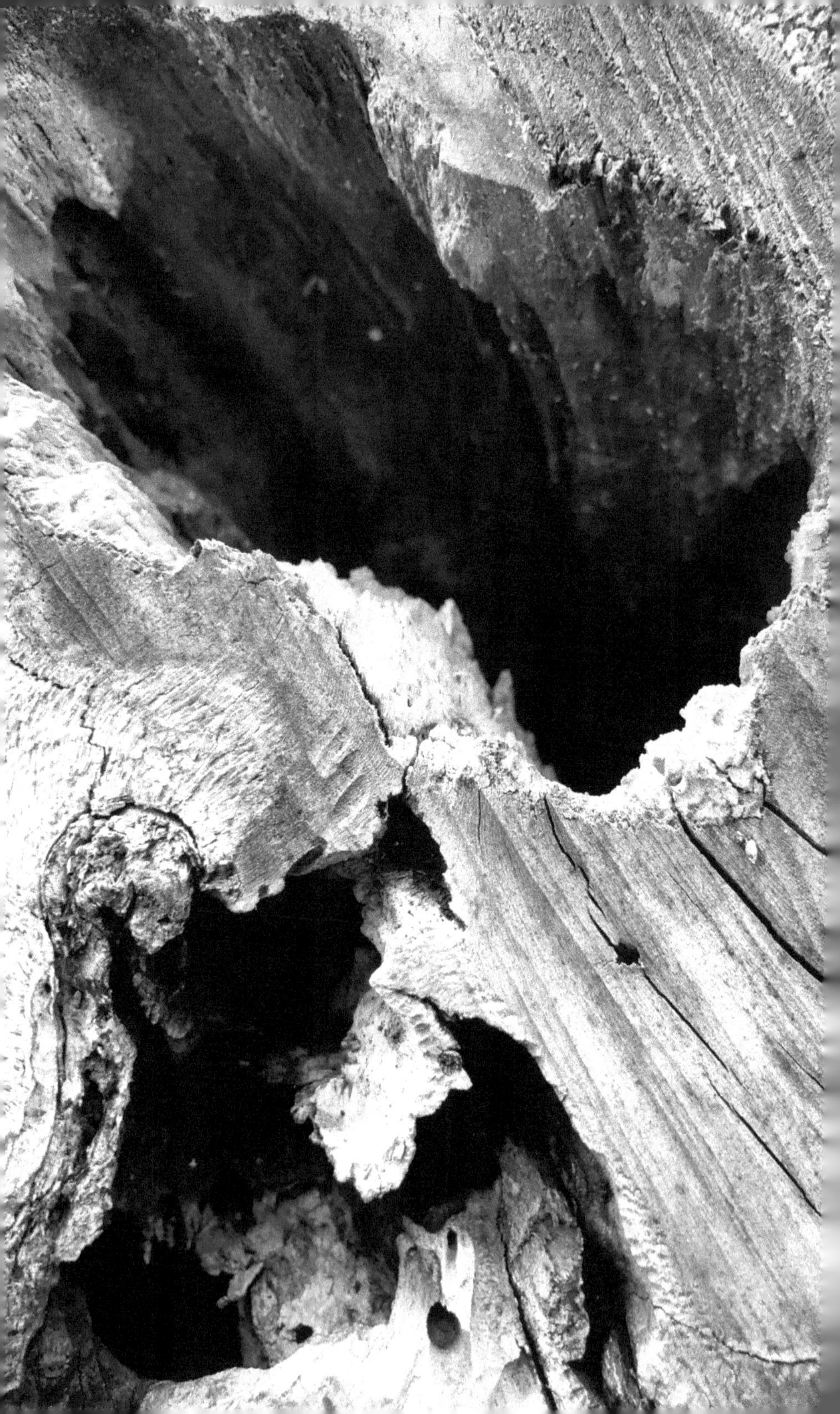

November First

I'm feeling a space; devoid; I'm a waste
An erasure of my life seems right
But the truth of the matter is, I'm needed in this place
By God and Jesus the Christ

J. Luke McClellan

November Second

My mental health feels helpless; bereft
No hope as my lows do take hold
I've belittled myself and still I can't rest
My woes I suppose will not go
So where is the inspiration to be found in this existence
I can't accept this concept; obsolete
Except there is one that I shall never forget
I'm reminded that in Christ, I'm complete

November Third

My location is changing
The sun rays hit my brow; such a sweat
My motivation is aging
I'm okay when I'm allowed to forget
So how do we save "we"
There's only one way in which can expect
His name begins with a Capital C
And ends with us willing to accept

J. Luke McClellan

November Fourth

Sometimes we part ways
For the best, it's okay
Let's admit that this life isn't it
And realize that the day
We will be able to say
In Christ, we're saved; life begins

Devotional Rhyme

November Fifth

The still waters still ripple
When movement contacts
The interaction is blissfully right
But with God's touch; literal
Things divine, come back
He is the land, sea and sky

J. Luke McClellan

November Sixth

The precious moments in nature do sing
The birds are at peace just to be
They communicate from afar, yet know who they are
All creations of our magnificent God; He
The Divine Creator of all things
His grandeur is unequivocally, never far

November Seventh

I can feel a distance in the venting of their rage
For they all think I am at fault
I begged and went to give my most honest display
Apologizing for what I had caused
But they rejected; unaccepted; sorrow declined
As they refused to renew and forgive
But in my essence, I guess it's, truly for the best
When I turned my other cheek as Christ did

J. Luke McClellan

November Eighth

The sounds in my head can be quite disturbing
I hear some voices calling me away
Not wanting to allow any thoughts said to be concerning
But I can't stop this noise in my brain
So how do I escape and calm and quell
This dramatic unfolding of events
I sit and I pray to God for His help
As I know He's the answer to this

Devotional Rhyme

November Ninth

The depths of my heart are far from the start
The beginning I was sent here to appeal
An innocence that was essentially secluded from the dark
Exactly how God intended us to be revealed
And yet somehow we instinctively would depart
From the Truth; the Light; the Real
And despite that fact, God still loves us back
No matter if we uphold our end of the deal

J. Luke McClellan

November Tenth

No one else is to blame
For the shame I do exclaim
A name I've indeed made for myself
For only I can create change
When I decide it's time to pray
And turn my life over to Christ for help

November Eleventh

We can frame our lives in a snapshot of time
But no one can capture the past
The ways that we tried; conveyed; but we deny
There's not a single clock's hand, we can turn back
So we shouldn't relapse, just leave it at that
Never to return as once was
Trust in the life, God has for us now; be glad
As only He can do what He does

J. Luke McClellan

November Twelfth

Moving without purpose
As humans often do
Why do we confide in apathy?
When it actually hurts us
To be so subdued
For we are the ones who are deceived
So let's let it be accepted
We're not doing our best it's
The truth we've removed from society
And may we all join hands to pray
For allowing God in our ways
To be at peace, in Jesus Christ, and He

November Thirteenth

∽

It seems impossibly challenging to face
That our world believes there's no hope
We continue to promote a narrow, self-seeking way
To live and it's for ourselves; alone
But knowing the unknown is quite honestly the thought
We need to embrace as our own
As we will never understand all of God's omnipotent,
magnificent ways
Yet, our faith in Him is our fate carved in stone

∽

J. Luke McClellan

November Fourteenth

The coals of this fire inside, burn with hot flames
Resulting in creating divine heat
The stones that they cast with a fantastic amount of disdain
And yet I am protected by He
For God is my solid rock and Jesus my iron shield
The armor I'm armed with today
Tomorrow, next week, month, year and decade
For in them, I've no end; not afraid

November Fifteenth

Apostasy has become a common theme
Amongst our society as one
Conglomeration of abominations; weak
We've decidedly accepted we're done
So how can we possibly stop these things
That we so adamantly succumb?
The truth is, Jesus forgives and still lives
In each of us, if that is what we want

J. Luke McClellan

November Sixteenth

I feel everyone has turned against me; hollow
Rejected; disconnected; spit out
They chewed my flesh to a fine paste to swallow
And this is the tolerance, I should allow?
I have to take a stand, dismissing such demands
Sending them back from whence they came
And yet that's just my emotion as only God knows when
It's appropriate for Him to go and exclaim

November Seventeenth

I'm seeking bridges to create passages to help me cross over gaps
The empty breaches in my mind's eye
But as I'm reaching for decisions to make as I think and in fact
I'm truly seeking much bigger than I
So why do I disguise my life in these lies
As I'm only depleting my time
Spending it offending and binging on a demise
As I now realize I can be renewed in a new life with Christ

J. Luke McClellan

November Eighteenth

My emptiness has existed since I spent it not living
For a life healed in God
My weaknesses seem to prevent how I want to be giving
For a life healed in God
But now I realize what I did and didn't wasn't or isn't
For a life healed in God
And now I confide that I am forgiven and absolved
For a life healed in God

November Nineteenth

I believe that the changes in me are greatly needed
As I've been seeking other things far too long
And I know that the flow of my river is downstream
If I continue to row my life in the wrong
Direction; unaffected; believing things I go do
Can't hurt me as I am too strong
But that's not the truth when the devil plays my tunes
Only in Christ can my heart prosper on

J. Luke McClellan

November Twentieth

Failure is a common, relatable theme
That no one in real life wants to admit to
Available social media is quite often the piece
That everyone unconsciously sings as strings of evil untruths
So why should we continue to feed
This devil-gleamed glitz we're subjected to?
Fill your time up with God and depart from evil's cause
Christ is the might we all need; our misery is proof

November Twenty-First

God continues to use me in unique ways
A reality that I can now see
I'm blessed to give my best, in His and Christ's name
As they're the essence of the heart of me

J. Luke McClellan

November Twenty-Second

If I'm being honest and sincere
I'm addicted to essentially near
Everything relating to dopamine
And my hope has been built
On my self-esteem, yet guilt
Seems to rob me of all my hopes and dreams
So where do I go
Once reaching the end of the road
The show can't go on like this
And out of my head I dream
That Jesus Christ wants me
And in fact that's a reality I can live

November Twenty-Third

This body of mine is beaten-down and aches
I'm sore to the core of my being
I'm seeking the wisdom I need to get from
God and Jesus as completing
The circle of my existence, not being existential
But they are the reason for my life
Every blessing inside from my heart to my mind
I'm aligned with my Heavenly Father and Christ

J. Luke McClellan

November Twenty-Fourth

God is reaching out to me, as I see all His signs
The way I've been living's been for me
And I need to abandon, the damning path of my mind
As this time, I'll get it right, living for He

November Twenty-Fifth

My mind's muscle I flex, is a blessing, yet I've left
All my faults alone at home to breathe
I see the cheapening of my selfishness; so helpless; bereft
As only God creates the peace, which I can achieve

J. Luke McClellan

November Twenty-Sixth

Trusting in God is the toughest of all
Simple in concept, yet hard
Such a shame to fall, when we deceive ourselves and all
The ways, we behave, when we aren't
Ready to engage in the peace He provides
Yet He resoundingly, effectively applies
Hope, despite our antics to avoid and dismantle it
God always is present in our lives

November Twenty-Seventh

※

May you purge the undeserving evil that has been
speakable in your words
For only God can restore lost hope
This demonic possession is evident in your being,
so demeaning
For only God can restore lost hope
And may you call upon Christ to strike down this strife
in your life
For only God can restore lost hope
Don't give up today, reverse these satanic ways
As God has been, and will always be, hope

※

J. Luke McClellan

November Twenty-Eighth

⸻

Writing for Christ is divine in the pen
Each stroke of the tip is so quick
Divinity, aplenty, I essentially many times lived
To get as my hope, which He gives

⸻

November Twenty-Ninth

God has called me a lot and I've ignored Him in thoughts
Living for me is what's hip
But it isn't so perplexing as the truest form of guessing
Is living this time without "it"
And "it" is defined as peace that's aligned
In God and Christ as my life
Yes, they know what's best as this world is a mess
So my time, with them is what's right

J. Luke McClellan

November Thirtieth

God blesses those He loves
With the peace of sleep
To dream and awaken again
Believe in what He does
Never to deceive
As Christ will free you of your sin

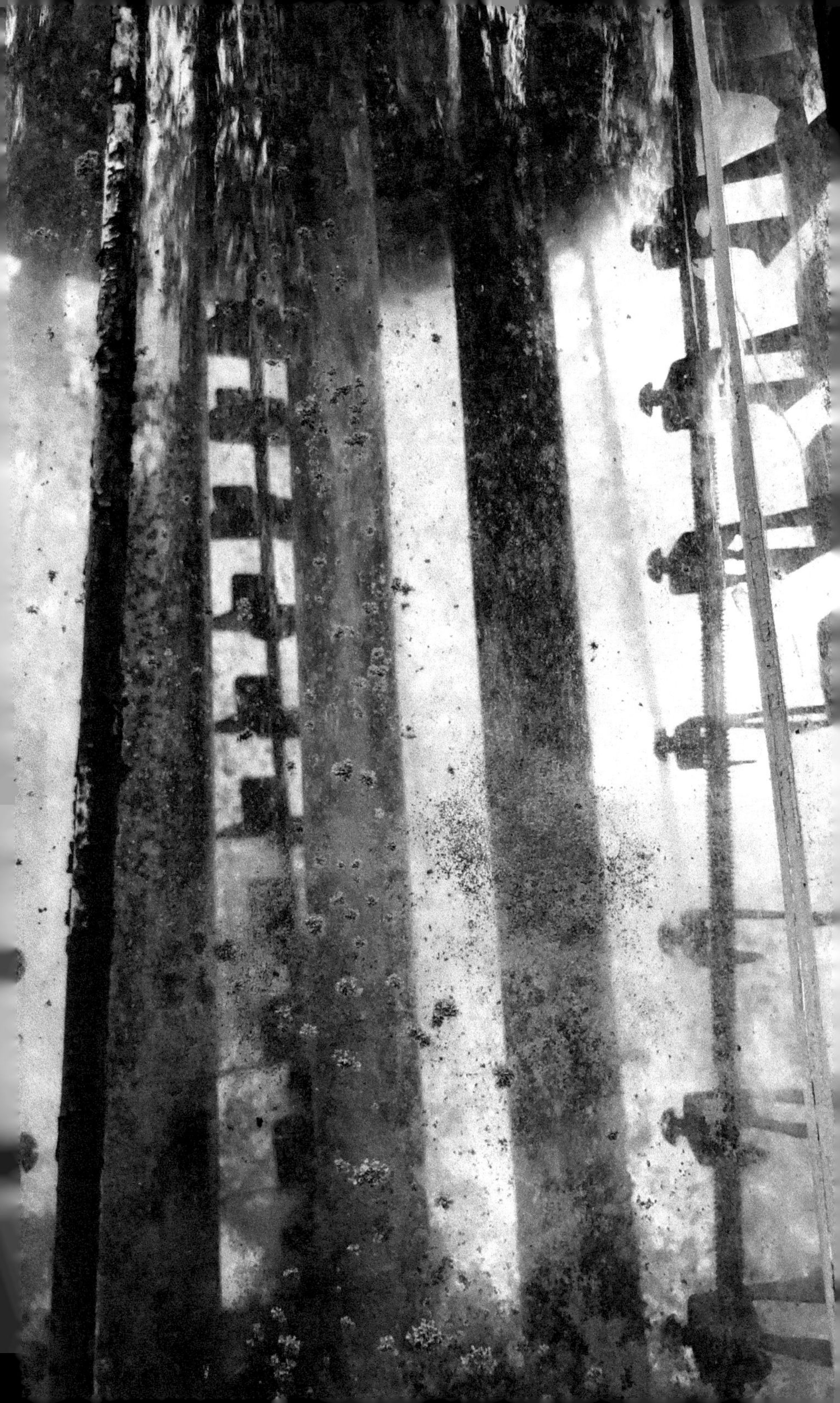

J. Luke McClellan

December First

My time is running out
Want to do something greater than just how
Everything I've been exposed to is what's right
The wrong is what's in
And it gets worse as the sin
Becomes what's common in our lives
So I deny the mainstream
As they seem to be making
Mistake after mistake and still try
To take me down the road to hell
But I'm not buying a ticket, so, oh well
I'm committing my life to God and Christ

December Second

As I'm washing away the pain that has sustained
Maintaining a place in my home
The throes I know God will overthrow; but I'm at odds
With the ways for which I've condoned
So I roam alone this nightly unknown
Alley of reality that's dark
Though God sees my deceit, He calls upon me to relieve
Myself from this hell and depart

J. Luke McClellan

December Third

The volume for which this switch has increased
I think I need to tone down
The deliberate, ignorant ways I have reached
Solve nothing as it hits to get me fowl
So how do I allow a new view that isn't skewed
If the ways for which I live, debilitate?
Talk more to God, as all is not lost
Yes, He and Christ Jesus are the way

December Fourth

God has solved all my enigmas in life
Isn't it though the sweetest discovery?
Yes He is all I need to get by
This is my receiving His love for me

J. Luke McClellan

December Fifth

My goodness I couldn't be any happier with God
He's given me so much of His love
He pushes me to feel the lasting applause
That's received from the leap of what I once was

December Sixth

My story is simple
I hurt and worked to not feel
But the glory's unequivocal
God heard and created my purpose; inner zeal

J. Luke McClellan

December Seventh

Tons of sleep
Is one of the things
Essential in feeling our best
But in order to achieve
Ask God and believe
We've received peace in He, as we rest

December Eighth

The addictions I've been in
Have prevented my livin'
Free in my life committed to Christ
I can't offer myself to Him
If for something else I'm pretendin'
But since then, I am free, and alive

J. Luke McClellan

December Ninth

Addiction is a common theme we as human beings seek
But the true drug we love is dopamine
And if we know this then we can get ahead of it without penalty
But it takes a force much greater than we think
As self-serving intentions are the pretensions we should leave
Yet our fault remains with "we"
So snap in your seatbelt and know we can be helped
And overcome all with God as our lead

December Tenth

Depression and emptiness are expecting us to be dismissed
The tones of the devil speak loud
And if we allow these weapons that teach and achieve perceived bliss
Then we are soon doomed, as the proud
So let's speak it aloud, as we go to avow
Such evil indeed lives in our lives
Now let's take out our towels and wipe the sweat from our brows
God is the resolution who can overcome our pride

J. Luke McClellan

December Eleventh

❦

We speak with emotion when we need to know when
The truth is above our own heads
As God is the hope in, all that's lost in the evil of sin
The belief in He is the proof of what's said

❦

December Twelfth

Existential reckoning is perplexingly affecting
Our society's mind; need variety
We die to see our minds at peace but wine and dine;
unleash the beast
Yes God is what's needed; our highest being

December Thirteenth

Too much individualism is what's destroying our humanism
The altruistic enlightenment is dead
For it has been said that with a single touch of God's hand who is the one
Single force that can repair, what was just said

December Fourteenth

So what else is left when we seek to please ourselves?
It's an empty road ahead if we continue on
The tale of all tales is good always prevails
God is the strength in us; divinely strong

J. Luke McClellan

December Fifteenth

༄

I tend to think we blink at each
Other then choose another; next
An endless cycle recycling humans; cheating
So who then do we seek
To end destroying our peace; yes?
He's called "God", the Omnipotent being

༄

December Sixteenth

The pain we live in this way
Is a change we should learn to pay
Attention to as you can guess who knows
God is aware of how we pray
And knows we want the despair erased
But we need to accept it and learn to grow

J. Luke McClellan

December Seventeenth

The experiences we have
God wants us to have
It's not about us; it's all for Him
We need to learn that
It's a concept for us to grasp
As our purpose is to be free from the sin

December Eighteenth

The time I've been allotted in my life
Is a time that only time will reveal
As God knows what's best, despite my perplexed
Feeling of despair at night
Daytime too as I kneel
Down at my bedside and confess

J. Luke McClellan

December Nineteenth

This life is not about what we want
Nor what we desire or need
It's about learning to be at peace with God
He wants us to not be stopped
As we seek out to achieve
Serving Him from reality to our thoughts

December Twentieth

The desires we embrace
Are the "liar's" deceptive ways
To tempt us, eventually to quit
And resign our love from Christ up above
But knowing this, we are the ones
With God, and can stop and prevent it

J. Luke McClellan

December Twenty-First

It's never enough as we always seek more
We receive and deplete and receive
It's never enough as we need more than before
But in God and Christ, of this, we are relieved

December Twenty-Second

We all get high from temptations in life
We all are indeed seeking a rush
But if it's never enough, then why do we buy
The devil's lies, yet in God we can trust?

J. Luke McClellan

December Twenty-Third

It may be too early
To say what is working
But my peace has indeed increased
Leaving behind burning
Sins of the flesh; yearning
Christ is my new way, which I believe

December Twenty-Fourth

Life's stairs are the steps
Which I don't want to take
The pain is egregious; my feet hurt
I stop in my thoughts; yet
Refuse to rest as I say
In God and Christ, my legs move to work

J. Luke McClellan

December Twenty-Fifth

Each second that ticks, as I sit here to get
A second chance at life; I aspire
To deny the evil, that the devil's path is
Attainable; as God's power is infinitely higher

December Twenty-Sixth

God has been waiting for this day
As I confide in Christ to say
"I submit God and give my life to you."
He smiles down upon my way
Knowing my truth, for which I state
Is the greatest gift I can give, and get too

J. Luke McClellan

December Twenty-Seventh

The Lord has provided, every ounce of good
That resides in my life on this earth
And for that I'm excited; my mouth speaks as it should
"Jesus Christ, the sacrifice that still works."

Devotional Rhyme

December Twenty-Eighth

It's impossible to please everyone
Even Christ, when here, was denied
God in the flesh, couldn't measure up
To the ways for which we want
As it's all about our current time
Yet God and Jesus, still treasure our love

J. Luke McClellan

December Twenty-Ninth

Our desperate attempts
To be relevant
Are in vain as everyone is the same
This world, we can't prevent
From encouraging the hell-centric
But with Jesus the Christ, we can abstain

December Thirtieth

The mark has been made
For which we should aim
Jesus is the love we could claim
Abandon sin today
And embrace all of Christ's ways
Yes in He, we indeed, can change

J. Luke McClellan

December Thirty-First

I know I must go
Leaving this show
The world may be swallowed up in flames
But I know what I know
And Christ is the hope
I need, to complete, my last days